CLASSIC

SERVING TRAYS

CLASSIC

Coca-Cola

SERVING TRAYS

BY ALLAN PETRETTI
& CHRIS H. BEYER

Very special recognition is extended to Phillip F. Mooney, Manager-Archives Department, and his staff at The Coca-Cola Company. Mr. Mooney provided the authors with extensive access to the archives and kindly offered his support and insights throughout the process of the development of this book.

ISBN: 0-930625-96-X
Library of Congress Catalog Card Number: 98-70852

Editor: Allan W. Miller
Designer: Chris Decker
Copy Editor: Sandra Holcombe
Editorial Assistant: Wendy Chia-Klesch

Printed in the United States of America

To order additional copies of this book or a catalog, please contact:

Antique Trader Books
P.O. Box 1050
Dubuque, Iowa 52004
1-800-334-7165

CONTENTS

INTRODUCTION
7

Chapter 1
THE BIRTH OF THE WORLD'S MOST FAMOUS SOFT DRINK
9

Chapter 2
MASS MERCHANDISING THROUGH EARLY PRINTING PROCESSES
17

Chapter 3
THE FIRST ISSUES OF COCA-COLA TRAYS: 1897-1910
25

Chapter 4
TRAY ISSUES OF THE YEARS 1911-1919
65

Chapter 5
TRAY ISSUES OF THE 1920s
77

Chapter 6
TRAY ISSUES OF THE 1930s
99

Chapter 7
TRAY ISSUES OF THE 1940s
117

Chapter 8
TRAY ISSUES OF THE 1950s AND 1960s
123

Chapter 9
ESSENTIAL INFORMATION FOR
COLLECTORS OF COCA-COLA TRAYS
139

Chapter 10
VIENNA ART PLATES
145

Chapter 11
COCA-COLA SERVING AND CHANGE TRAY RARITY OVERVIEW
155

COCA-COLA TRAY PRICE GUIDE
159

BIBLIOGRAPHY
165

The Louisville, Kentucky, Bottling Company used this promotional truck in a 1932 door-to-door campaign to promote the use of Coca-Cola. Purchasers of a six-bottle carton of Coca-Cola received a free Coca-Cola serving tray and an ice pick. The truck is pictured in front of the bottling plant. This type of advertising promotion demonstrates the fact that the Coca-Cola Company promoted its product on all fronts—direct to the consumer, through soda fountains, and anywhere the Coca-Cola drink could be merchandised.

INTRODUCTION

Coca-Cola® advertising and serving trays were used by The Coca-Cola Company for a period of nearly seventy years to merchandise and promote their celebrated soft drink, which has become a worldwide phenomenon. These trays are wonderful historical reminders of a by-gone era, spanning a period from the mid-1890s through 1961, and they have become prized collectors' items. The colorful images printed on the serving trays of The Coca-Cola Company provide a remarkable visual diary of fashions and objects which typified styles and helped shape lasting impressions of our past. Equally fascinating, of course, is the history and development of The Coca-Cola Company itself.

The early years of The Coca-Cola Company paralleled three other historically significant developments. First, there was the emergence of the advertising specialty industry, which promoted the use of printed signs and a variety of other materials in the mass promotion of products. Second, was the technological development of productive printing processes, which made it possible to duplicate printing onto a variety of surfaces. Third, was the exploding popularity of the soda fountain, where tasty flavored sodas were served in pleasant surroundings to an eager and receptive public.

These important historical developments of the late 1800s helped The Coca-Cola Company to achieve its well-chronicled and extraordinary growth. Any study or examination of Coca-Cola serving trays as advertising art must, therefore, include a discussion of each of these topics. While not intended to provide a complete and definitive history of The Coca-Cola Company, this book will offer an overview of the exciting and formative years of the company, devoting particular attention to early contributions in merchandising and promotion. Also examined herein will be the formative years of advertising promotion as a business in the United States, along with the printing methods that helped make the use of mass produced print media advertising possible. Finally, a detailed discussion and pictographic examination of each Coca-Cola tray is included.

Who is this book for? It is for anyone interested in learning about early Coca-Cola advertising memorabilia. It will also appeal to anyone desiring fresh, new information about the early years of The Coca-Cola Company, specifically how the firm effectively used innovative merchandising techniques to catapult to the worldwide success enjoyed today. It is also for those who simply find the beautiful imagery of Coca-Cola trays an appropriate subject for examination and enjoyment on the basis of artistic merit. And, it is a book that should delight anyone intrigued by the development of printed-image advertising in America. Indeed, this is a book for any and all who share an interest in the world's most widely recognized and renowned soft drink!

Jacobs' Pharmacy, which was located at Five Points in Atlanta, Georgia, in the 1880s. It was here that Dr. John S. Pemberton took his formula for a new medicinal elixir which he called "French Wine of Coca" for its first production in July 1887.

CHAPTER ONE

THE BIRTH OF THE WORLD'S MOST FAMOUS SOFT DRINK

Mankind has always searched for magic elixirs to cure ills and restore youthful zest. This quest reached widespread proportions in the United States during the industrial revolution, and lasted until shortly after the turn of the century, when the food and drug administration began regulating the pharmaceutical industry. Tonics, many of which included a high percentage of alcohol, were touted for their medicinal qualities believed to be capable of relieving symptoms such as bilious headache, dyspepsia, blood disorders, exhaustion, and an endless variety of ills. Trade names of these cure-all formulas in the 1880s included: Indian Root Bitters, Dr. Richardson's Tonic, Rex Bitters, Wa-Hoo Bitters, and a multitude of others. Some of these products were the result of a genuine effort to minimize the side effects of illnesses. Most, however, merely provided an easy way to make money. With no laws governing truth in advertising, it was difficult to know if one was buying a medicine that would help improve one's health, or a trumped-up alcoholic beverage from a "snake oil" salesman.

It was in this period that a pharmacist from Atlanta developed the formula which ultimately became Coca-Cola. In 1885, Dr. John S. Pemberton concocted a medicinal elixir which he called "French Wine of Coca." It is alleged that Pemberton omitted alcohol from the formula and added other essences resulting in a tasty, dark brown syrup drink. Sensing that he might have a beverage with public appeal, Pemberton took his syrup drink to Jacob's Pharmacy which, at the time, was a large successful business in Atlanta. By 1886, he convinced the owner to offer the drink at his location as a refreshment for customers.

At some point early on, it was suggested that Pemberton should add carbonated soda water to the syrup. After a successful debut of the syrup and soda water blend, a new drink was born. Frank M. Robinson, Pemberton's accountant, is credited with recommending that the drink be called Coca-Cola. Robinson is also attributed the distinction of having designed the fancy script Coca-Cola® trademark, which has since become synonymous with the drink. That name would become a registered trademark some seven years later, in 1893.

An oil cloth sign was soon placed on the side of Jacob's Pharmacy advertising the new drink. The first known print advertisement for Coca-Cola was a small ad in the May 26, 1886, issue of the *Atlanta Journal.* The first promotional ad copy for Coca-Cola used words such as "Delicious, Refreshing, Invigorating" to describe the beverage. During the same year, advertising tickets, providing opportunities for new customers to try the drink, were also used. Right from the start, Coca-Cola was merchandised at five cents per drink. Wooden syrup barrels were shipped and sold to retailers with the bright Coca-Cola logo and distinctive trademark painted on them.

Coca-Cola was not an early success, however. Only twenty-five gallons were sold in 1886. Pemberton had spent far more on promotion and advertising than he had recovered in sales! Further compounding matters was Pemberton's failing health. At 56 years of age, having neither the resources nor time to promote his new drink, Pemberton sold the majority of his interest in Coca-Cola to several investors. Asa G. Candler, also an Atlanta pharmacist, bought the remaining interest Pemberton had in Coca-Cola in 1888. Later that year, Candler located the other investors and bought them out, gaining sole and complete controlling interest in the Coca-Cola Beverage enterprise. For a total investment of $2,300, Candler owned the secret formula for Coca-Cola and the equipment to produce it. Sadly, Pemberton was never able to see the success of his drink. He died the same year in which his investment in Coca-Cola was sold to Candler.

Candler's timing was impeccable. Several years before the development of Coca-Cola, a new concept caught fire at the 1876 Centennial Exposition in Philadelphia. In order to provide refreshment to the thousands who attended the event from all over the country, booths were constructed which offered refreshing mineral waters and seltzers. A few short years after the Philadelphia Exposition, the phenomenon known as soda fountains began appearing in cities throughout the United States—establishments where non-alcoholic beverages and ice cream were served in clean and pleasant surroundings. By the mid-1880s, the soda fountain had become an established American institution. These commercial enterprises provided the ideal place to promote a variety of beverages.

The very earliest advertising promotion included drink tickets, horse-drawn wagons with advertising signs, and newspaper advertisements in the towns and cities of the South, where Coca-Cola was offered at soda fountains. By 1890, the drink was rapidly catching on. Encouraged by this early success, Candler forged ahead with his new enterprise.

Candler was both a visionary and a promoter. In 1891, the first known advertising calendar for Coca-Cola referred to the new drink as: "A delightful summer or winter drink. For headache or tired feeling. Relieves mental and physical exhaustion." The calendar listed the business name as Asa G. Candler & Co., Atlanta, Georgia. Other merchandising items used by Candler included free drink tickets, advertising clocks, and ceramic syrup urns which included the Coca-Cola logo and a promotional slogan. The first printed paper advertising sign was also ordered in 1891, for distribution in a quantity of 500. Harkening back to its beginnings in a pharmacy, Coca-Cola was marketed in its formative years as a refreshing drink having medicinal properties. The earliest promotion slogans included "The ideal Brain Tonic, specific for headache," while other ads used one-word descriptions such as "invigorating" and "exhilarating".

By 1892, Candler founded The Coca-Cola Company, which was initially capitalized at $100,000. Candler was joined in the venture by his brother and a few other investors. Sensing the continuing need to grow the business through promotion, the first enameled-metal advertising sign was used in 1893. Another big boost to Coca-Cola was its availability and promotion at the Chicago World's Fair that same year. This event proved to be a fantastic opportunity, as the unique taste of Coca-Cola was experienced by people from all regions of the country.

The business took off, and by 1895 sales offices in Chicago, Los Angeles, Dallas, and Philadelphia were operating. Advertising expenditures had increased from $46 in 1886 to $17,744 in 1895. Although that figure seems trivial by today's standards, it must be remembered that printed tin signs were purchased from early tin lithographers for just a few cents each! Coca-Cola started another advertising tradition at this time: Large colorful signs were painted on the sides of buildings. Already, the company's merchandising strategy was evident. Asa Candler wanted the Coca-Cola trademark to be visible everywhere. By 1895, the firm's internal annual report stated that Coca-Cola was sold, in some quantity, in every state of the Union.

While Asa Candler envisioned Coca-Cola as a soda fountain drink, one of his customers saw things differently. Joseph A. Biedenharn, who sold Coca-Cola at his soda fountain in Vicksburg, Mississippi, was convinced that Coca-Cola would enjoy success as a take-along drink at picnics and other social events. In 1895, he began using a bottle design known as the Hutchinson bottle to encapsulate carbonated Coca-Cola. This design had a permanent stopper affixed in the neck of the bottle which, when pushed down into the bottle, allowed a customer to consume the beverage. Even when Biedenharn achieved some initial success with his concept, Candler remained uninterested in bottling his drink in this manner.

Perhaps one reason that Asa Candler wasn't interested in bottling Coca-Cola was that he was having such great success selling Coca-Cola syrup to soda fountains—annual sales totaled 281,055 gallons by 1899. In the same year, two lawyers named Benjamin Franklin Thomas and Joseph Brown Whitehead, from Chattanooga, Tennessee, also had an interest in the concept of bottling Coca-Cola. They met with Asa Candler in an unsuccessful attempt to gain bottling rights to the beverage. After further discussions, however, Candler agreed to give them sole bottling rights for Coca-Cola in most areas of the United States. The only exceptions to their granted territories were a few New England states, and certain portions of Texas and Mississippi. Shortly following the execution of this agreement, the first officially sanctioned bottling of Coca-Cola began in 1899.

This prominent building, located at 47 Peachtree St., in Atlanta, was where Asa G. Candler produced Coca-Cola Syrup from September 1888 until 1891. Candler obtained controlling interest in Coca-Cola in 1888 from Dr. John S. Pemberton, whose health was failing, and from other investors.

The arrangement between these two lawyers and Candler was simple. They would purchase syrup from The Coca-Cola Company, and subsequently bottle it. Although it would appear that Candler lost a significant opportunity in this arrangement, he would benefit greatly from it, over time, by being the exclusive controlling seller of the syrup. Thus, the relationship of the parent company (The Coca-Cola Company) and the regional bottlers began. Early on, Thomas and Whitehead had different ideas about how the business should be run, and they split their franchise areas into two regions throughout the United States. Thomas assumed most of the North and East, along with the Pacific Coast, while Whitehead assumed the deep

South and Southwest, Midwest, and areas to the Pacific Coast. These two companies then began to function as parent bottlers.

The two original parent bottlers later established regional bottlers in their territories, including Western Coca-Cola bottling in Chicago, The Coca-Cola Bottling Company in Atlanta, and The Coca-Cola Bottling Company in Dallas. These regional bottlers were added just after the turn of the century. In turn, the regional bottlers added numerous other local bottlers and, by 1909, Coca-Cola had 379 bottlers operating throughout the United States. Thus, the foundation of a distribution network was firmly established, and this would allow the company to grow and expand.

Within this distribution system, the function of The Coca-Cola Company of Atlanta was twofold: First, to provide sales and promotional direction for the merchandising of Coca-Cola; second, the Company retained control of syrup sales to bottlers and to jobbers who, in turn, serviced the fountain service business.

As fountain sales continued to boom, the bottling business took off as well. The original Hutchinson bottles used from 1895 to 1901 were replaced by bottles that could be sealed with a metal cap. By 1910, sales of Coca-Cola Syrup totaled 4.2 million gallons. Whether found in a bottle or at a soda fountain, Coca-Cola was becoming available everywhere.

From its inception, The Coca-Cola Company displayed a remarkable understanding of the power of merchandising. Coca-Cola was promoted through the use of colorful signs, calendars, bookmarks, soda fountain serving trays, tickets, large signs on buildings, thermometers, fans, and an endless array of items viewed and used by the public in everyday life. Each passing year in the company's early history witnessed the introduction and use of new merchandising concepts.

An early and major advertising development—and more importantly, one which is central to the subject of this book—took place in 1896. Franklin Garrett, who served as the Coca-Cola Archivist for many years, wrote and compiled *The Black Book/History of Coca-Cola 1886-1940*. This invaluable but unpublished reference provides a wealth of information about the Company's history. In the *Black Book*, Garrett records that the first advertising serving tray was used in 1896. The importance of that notation, and the mystery it provides, will be revealed later when the entire subject of Coca-Cola serving trays is discussed.

Other interesting developments in the early promotion of Coca-Cola included the use of the first advertising window display, in 1899. In 1902, the first advertisement of Coca-Cola appeared in the national publication, *Munsey Magazine*. That same year, the company purchased its first automobile (actually a truck) to promote its product. By 1903, hundreds of thousands of signs, serving trays, and other merchandising items were in widespread circulation. Perhaps the most effective advertising promotional item of all was the printed free drink ticket, which was distributed at soda fountains and printed in magazines and newspapers.

While tickets were used from the beginning to entice people to try the "Delicious and Refreshing" Coca-Cola drink, the program of directly reimbursing soda fountains for free drinks provided to fulfill printed ticket offers began in 1897. This strategy was a brilliant one. Millions of free Coca-Cola drinks had been distributed throughout the country. The company reimbursed ticket certificates to soda fountains and other vendors for a total of

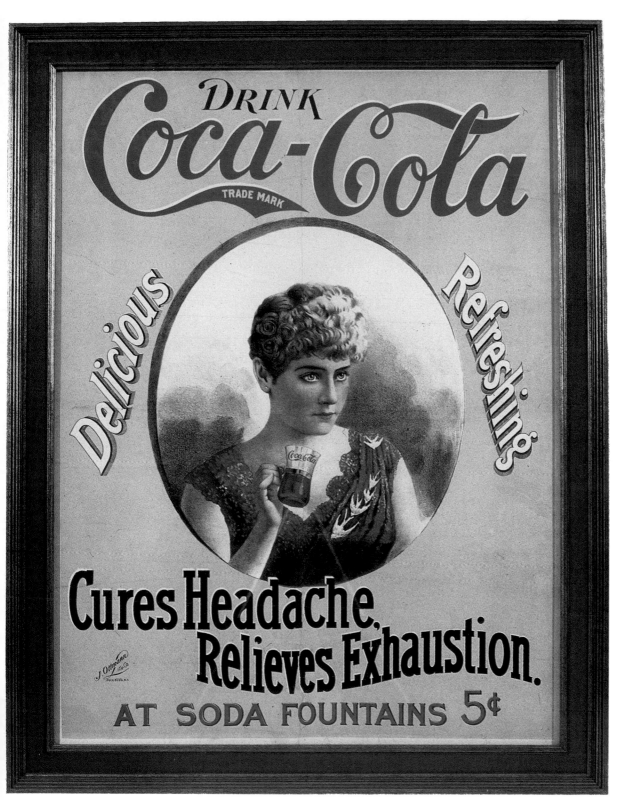

1896 Cameo paper sign, 30" by 40", printed by J. Ottman Lith. Co., NY. This image was used on at least one calendar and a number of signs in 1896. However, a serving tray featuring this charming lady has never been found.

$19,618 in 1897. By 1908, that amount had increased to $33,894. The repeated use of massive amounts of advertising promotion devices and free drink tickets helped create and solidify the market position of "America's Drink." Early on in the soda drink saga, The Coca-Cola Company had left its numerous competitors and imitators in the dust.

Coca-Cola engaged the use of advertising specialists before the turn of the century. In the first years, Candler used the services of an Atlanta-based advertising agency known as the Massengale Company. In 1906, the D'Arcy Company of St. Louis, Missouri, was selected to provide advertising services to Coca-Cola, and this firm remained the company's primary advertising agency for many years. Candler had a heavy hand in directing the look of early Coca-Cola advertising. He and his associate, Frank Mason Robinson, favored the use of attractive young female faces and figures to promote their product. Early calendars and serving trays all portrayed the visages of beautiful young women.

By 1904, Coca-Cola was becoming a household word throughout the country. National circulation magazines such as *The Ladies Home Journal* and *The Saturday Evening Post* displayed large Coca-Cola advertisements on their back covers. Dime novels, which were also popular at the time, exhibited promotional advertising for Coca-Cola on their back covers as well. Advertising themes and slogans were consistent, and carried through on all merchandising items. Early print advertisements showed Coca-Cola serving trays being used to serve Coca-Cola in soda fountains. In 1906, Coca-Cola had an astounding advertising budget (for that time) of $500,000. Just six years later, the annual advertising budget for The Coca-Cola Company exceeded one million dollars.

The years 1910-1920 witnessed the growth of Coca-Cola beyond the borders of the United States and into foreign countries. By 1912, Coca-Cola was even sold in Japan. There were 691 bottlers throughout the United States that same year. Detailed reports of advertising expenses in 1913 demonstrated how massive the merchandising program for Coca-Cola really was. Collectors of Coca-Cola advertising memorabilia will marvel at the number of items produced and, even more importantly, wonder where all these colorful advertising pieces are today. The following is just a small portion of the list of advertising items distributed by The Coca-Cola Company to its bottlers and fountain service customers in 1913, as listed in *The Black Book/History of Coca-Cola 1886-1940*.

Quantity	Advertising items distributed in 1913
5,000,000	Lithographed tin signs, in a variety of sizes
2,000,000	Serving trays for soda fountains
1,000,000	Calendars
200,000	4-head cutouts for window display
10,000,000	Matchbooks
250,000	Special signs for bottlers

While fountain sales still reigned in 1917, bottle sales were rapidly approaching the numbers that fountain sales were generating. In that year, syrup sales totaled 10,000,000 gallons for the first time. Shortly thereafter, the number of franchised bottlers totaled 1,095. There were also 1,871 jobbers who delivered syrup to soda fountains in the United States. The company trained soda fountain owners to properly merchandise the product for maximum sales effectiveness. Coca-Cola also went to great lengths to insure that its vendors carefully observed company guidelines for purity and sanitation in serving the drink.

The combination of a national network of bottling plants, a growing fountain service business, and a sophisticated mass merchandising program, helped to build a soft drink empire. What John S. Pemberton had conceived as a tonic drink in 1886, Asa G. Candler was able to merchandise into a worldwide popular beverage. Candler's $2,300 investment in Coca-Cola paid off in such spectacular proportions that he was able to sell the company for the astounding sum of $25,000,000 in 1919.

Ernest Woodruff, an Atlanta Banker, and a group of other investors visualized even greater accomplishments for the company. Soon after their purchase, the company was reincorporated and stock was offered to the public. The Woodruff family intended to build upon the foundation Candler had laid, and lead the company to even loftier heights.

During the same period in which The Coca-Cola Company was establishing its dominance in the category of soft drinks, the world of advertising communication was exploding. To fully examine and understand the pivotal role serving trays played in the early merchandising of Coca-Cola, it is important to first explore the development of mass merchandising through the use of print advertising.

The first printed advertisement for Coca-Cola appeared in the Atlanta Journal on May 29, 1886. It displayed the copy slogan "Delicious! Refreshing! Exhilarating! and Invigorating!" —words used for decades in describing what would become the most famous soft drink in the world.

CHAPTER TWO

MASS MERCHANDISING THROUGH EARLY PRINTING PROCESSES

A s noted in the introduction, the beginnings of The Coca-Cola Company in the late 1880s coincided with the emergence of important developments in America. First, the new phenomenon of the commercial soda fountain was started in that period. At the same time, merchandisers began to make use of a variety of visual media to advertise their products. And, by the 1890s, the printing of multiple colors on tin became both possible and profitable—the result of innovative new printing processes. These events all became intertwined, and helped to propel The Coca-Cola Company into an amazing period of growth and development.

With the advent of technologies which allowed printing on tin surfaces, producers of beer, liquor, tobacco, and flavored soda waters quickly realized the potential benefits of using brightly colored tin signs to advertise their wares. Coca-Cola proved to be decades ahead of its contemporaries in this endeavor and, as was so often the case, its enlightened marketing strategies helped to define the process of mass advertising used in this society.

From the perspective of living in the closing years of the Twentieth Century, it is difficult to imagine a world without electronic communications technology. Lacking the communication marvels of radio and television, advertisers at the turn of the century used the process of lithographic printing to promote products. Although small quantities of tin and paper advertising signs were produced in the 1870s and 1880s, the refined technology needed to manufacture high-quality printed tin signs in mass quantities was not yet available. Fortunately for Coca-Cola enthusiasts everywhere, the development of tin lithography, and the formative years of print advertising, precisely paralleled the first years of The Coca-Cola Company.

Historical documents from The Coca-Cola Company archives indicate that the first serving tray was produced for the Company in 1896. The picture at left shows the top portion of a calendar dated 1897. Artwork matching this calendar top was the subject of the first known Coca-Cola tray produced.

"Specialty Advertising" as a trade was an idea first conceived by a printer named William Shaw, who operated a business out of Coshocton, Ohio. By the late 1880s, Shaw had developed a successful business printing small advertising trade cards. These colorful cards used attractive, interesting, and sometimes humorous graphics to promote a variety of products. Trade cards were the earliest kinds of mass-produced, and colorful, printed advertising items. Today, these early forms of mass advertising are highly sought after as collector's items.

About the same time, two competing Coshocton, Ohio, newspapermen sensed the potential for "Novelty" advertising items as well. J. F. Meek and H. D. Beach expanded their newspaper businesses to include Specialty Advertising. Meek developed the idea, in 1887, of printing colorful advertisements on school bags. With instant success at hand, Meek saw the potential for a variety of other mass-use items to serve as advertising subjects. These included the backs of chairs, thermometers, newspaper bags, grocery aprons, fans, and calendars. Meek's new company was named the Tuscarora Advertising Company.

In 1888, H. D. Beach entered the advertising specialty business with a firm known as the Standard Advertising Company. Originally, this company's biggest business involved the production of advertising calendars. Both companies flourished, and the number of items offered as advertising media was expanded to include such objects as rulers, yardsticks, thermometers, and memoranda books. Soon, both of these firms added sales representatives, and began producing advertising items throughout the entire country. These two enterprising companies played a pivotal role—leading the way for American businesses to employ a wide variety of everyday items for the display of merchandising messages.

It was H. D. Beach who persevered in the process of developing methods to productively print on metal. Beach was attributed with being the first to use a power steam press to reproduce printed images onto metal signs. By 1890, more advertising specialty companies, including the Charles W. Shonk Company of Chicago and the Kaufmann & Strauss Company of New York, entered into the production of tin lithography. These two firms were thought to have followed Beach's lead by introducing power presses to their manufacturing operations in the early 1890s, with the specific purpose of producing printed tin advertising signs. By 1896, the Tuscarora Advertising Company also moved into the technology of lithography-on-metal.

By March of 1901, the two rival advertising companies (Standard and Tuscarora) merged, forming the Meek and Beach Company. Beach soon withdrew from the newly formed company, and subsequently started his own firm known as the H. D. Beach Company. Meek dropped the reference to Beach by 1905, simply calling his firm the Meek Company. This company prospered in the advertising specialty field, with the manufacture of celluloid items, calendars, and tin advertising. By 1909, Meek changed the company name to American Art Works, which would endure until 1950, when the company ceased operations.

EARLY ADVERTISING, AND THE FIRST SERVING TRAYS

The early years of the Advertising Specialty business have been discussed here to illustrate how the evolution of the advertising industry paralleled the formative years of The Coca-Cola Company. The first use of advertising serving trays began within ten years of both the founding of The Coca-Cola Company and the development of a productive process for printing advertising on metal surfaces. No single promotional item would serve such a long-lasting or prominent use in The Coca-Cola Company's merchandising program as did the serving tray.

With the emergence of the soda fountain and the explosion of the beer bottling industry, an advertising piece which could also function as a serving tray in a saloon or soda fountain was a natural. Soda fountains were opening in major cities throughout the country, and many of the fountains were combined with existing pharmacy businesses. Coca-Cola quickly sensed that serving trays could provide the perfect vehicle to promote their "delicious and refreshing" beverage in a soda fountain setting. No one knows the exact date in which the first beverage serving tray was produced, but the earliest examples of liquor and soda serving trays were thought to have been manufactured by the Tuscarora Advertising Company in the mid- to late 1890s. There are no known design patents, and the very earliest trays were not dated.

Serving trays were produced in a wide variety of sizes and shapes. Most were oval or rectangular, with some being round as well. All trays had curled edges for the presumed purpose of keeping soda or beer from spilling off the tray. Serving trays were generally 10 1/2 inches by 13 1/4 inches, or larger. Another important tray design is the "tip" or "change" tray. These trays were not large enough to serve drinks, but were made to return the customer's change, and to retain the server's tip. A common size for oval tip trays was 4 1/2 inches by 6 1/2 inches. Still other change or tip trays were round, with 4-inch and 6-inch diameters.

Early soda fountains played a large part in the success of Coca-Cola's rapid growth as a favored soft drink. This example shows advertising dating from the ceramic urn (mid-1890s) through the 1920s. The fountain equipment was typical of that seen around the turn of the century.

Both the larger serving trays, and smaller tip trays, were particularly functional advertising mediums which provided the fountain service with a convenient way to serve Coca-Cola and to return the customer's change. The Coca-Cola Company's widespread use of serving trays resulted in distribution of some 80 different trays, spanning a period of nearly seventy years. The beautiful artwork used for the trays, and the range in fashions depicted on them for over seven decades, makes for a truly exciting field of collecting. As noted earlier, before the illustrated advertising tray could come into existence, a process for printing onto metal had to be designed and developed. The printing technologies which came to the forefront during the first years of The Coca-Cola Company made the existence and use of the advertising-imprinted serving tray possible. Collectors, and those interested in early advertising and serving trays, will be well served in understanding the printing processes which resulted in the serving tray's production.

THE PROCESS OF PRINTING ON SERVING TRAYS

Much has changed since the initial process of printing onto metal surfaces was developed. The first such printing process used as many as twenty separate press runs to produce colors or tones, and the trays themselves had to be shaped and formed. Consequently, the earliest process used to produce trays was extraordinarily involved and very labor intensive. In sharp contrast, today's photolithography process is highly automated, with computer enhancements and highly efficient methods for reproducing a virtual rainbow of colors and tonal variations. In order to fully understand and appreciate differences in the appearance of early trays as contrasted with their later-day counterparts, a more detailed explanation of the printing processes and methods is necessary.

CHROMO-LITHOGRAPHY

The earliest process used to print images onto metal is known as chromo-lithography, a variation of the lithography printing process discovered by Aloys Senefelder, a German printer, in the 1790s. Chromo-lithography, because it employed limestone plates to transfer *printing* images to *printed* images, is also referred to as "stone lithography." In the most basic terms, the lithographic printing process is based on the well-known premise that oil and water don't mix. Here's how the process worked:

First, an artist drew colored images onto a limestone offset plate with special lithographic crayons containing an oil-based ink. Once the images were drawn onto the plate, water was applied over the entire surface. Printing ink, which would naturally adhere to the oil-based image area (as defined by the artist's lithographic crayons), but not to the water-coated remainder of the plate, was then applied. Paper could then be placed directly onto the plate, allowing the ink to transfer onto the paper, thereby creating a printed impression.

This process, which worked well for printing onto paper, was not a very effective way to print on metal. Metal is quite inflexible, and is usually not perfectly smooth or flat. Consequently, when an inked-image limestone plate was applied to a metal surface, irregularities in ink coverage usually occurred, resulting in less-than-crisp images. The first printed metal advertising signs produced in the early 1890s lacked in quality due to this problem. But, a solution to this vexing situation was soon to be discovered.

The Meek Company, in the mid-1890s, worked with a local firm to develop a highly effective method of actually printing onto metal—an adaptation of the process known as "offset" lithography. It was discovered that crisp printed images could be achieved by using

This colorful 1900 calendar (left) features the same image as serving and change trays issued that same year (above). Over the years, nineteen calendars depicted the same art as serving trays which were distributed as advertising collateral to promote Coca-Cola. An interesting focus in collecting these timeless reminders of early advertising would be to collect both the serving trays and the calendars with matching artwork.

This picture is the one used to create the artwork for the Hilda Clark pieces.

a rubber "blanket" as an intermediate—or "offset"—surface to transfer ink images to the surface of the metal. In effect, rubber had the flexibility to be compatible with a variety of surfaces, be they metal, limestone, or paper. As a result, a process had been developed which would allow for quality metal lithography.

"Offset presses" were the devices used to implement the lithographic printing on metal. The lithographic stone was affixed to a flat area (bed) of the press. The bed was capable of moving in a horizontal motion, so that ink rollers on the press could apply ink to the plate. The image would then be transferred to a rubber "blanket" mounted on a cylinder. The metal blank (the item to be printed to) would then be fed into the press, and the image from the rubber blanket would be transferred to its surface. The now-printed blank would then be taken to a drying station to await application of the next color and image. Once all the colors and images were applied, the printed item would be ready for use.

Use of the chromo-lithography process meant that a new printing plate had to be created for each primary color and shade of color. Many of the more complex pictures required as many as twenty separate runs through the press! If a registration or alignment problem occurred during any of the runs, the item was thrown away. When the signs or trays were printed properly, a final clear lacquer coat was applied for protection from the elements—after all, many of the signs were to be used outdoors, on the sides of buildings. The finished products of this type of printing are truly works of art. Color definition and the depth provided by separate runs for each subtle shade resulted in pieces that are absolutely stunning in their vivid imagery. Many consider these treasures highly superior to trays manufactured after stone lithography was replaced as a printing method by more productive photo-lithography.

Once the flat serving tray blanks were printed, they were shaped or sized by a stamping die press. In still another operation, which required a drawing press, the lip of the tray was formed. In the final production step, the trays were transferred to a press, which curled the lip of the tray. At long last, the serving tray was ready for distribution and use. Clearly, this entire process was incredibly labor intensive. Nevertheless, in spite of the arduous human involvement and many manufacturing steps, The Coca-Cola Company paid only a few cents each for the earliest trays. Hundreds of thousands of trays were made for soda manufacturers, breweries, and other advertisers using this early process. It is easy to see why the reproduction of serving trays using the same methods as were used for the originals would be cost prohibitive today. Further, it is doubtful that any of the printing equipment used to make the original trays still exists.

PHOTO-LITHOGRAPHY

Around 1900, a much more efficient and less labor intensive printing method was discovered. This process used photographic processes to obtain a set of color separations to be used in platemaking. Only four color plates were needed in the printing process—cyan, magenta, yellow, and black—leading to much shorter total press run times. Through photography, a microscopic etched-dot pattern of the image to be reproduced was formed on each printing plate or stone. The relative size and dispersion of these tiny dots provided the ability to achieve a wide variety of tones and shades in the final printed product. And, as has been already noted, all of this could be accomplished in only four press runs. This process proved to be inherently faster and more cost effective than chromo-lithography.

Shorter drying times between runs; fewer colors and shades to print (translating to fewer press runs); and a diminished chance of registration errors, all added up to significant improvements. The process progressed even further in later years, when superior-quality zinc plates replaced the traditional limestone plates.

The improved productivity of this refined process, combined with new presses running as much as seven times faster than the old flat bed presses, relegated stone, or chromo-lithography, to the status of a dying and lost art. Most printers of advertising trays began converting to photo-lithography in the teens. All of the Coca-Cola serving trays after the 1914 Betty tray designs were produced with photo-lithography. American Artworks, however, continued to use more than four colors in their printing processes up into the 1930s.

The trained eye can easily distinguish a chromolithography tray from a photo-lithography tray. Early stone litho printed trays, including those produced for Coca-Cola through 1914, exhibit large color separation dots and the incomparable deep multi-colors that resulted from separate color runs for each individual shade. Most of the later photo-lithography printed trays exhibit a fine dot screen pattern (when viewed under modest magnification)—the result of using four photographically-produced and screened color separations. The depth of color on the original stone litho trays is simply spectacular. The later trays are very attractive, of course, but they lack the deep, rich appearance of the pre-1914 trays.

THE PRINTERS

Over the years, nine firms are known to have printed serving and tip trays for The Coca-Cola Company. Those firms include Standard Advertising Company; Meek and Beach Co.; Charles W. Shonk Co., Chicago; The Meek Company; N. Y. Metal Ceiling Company; H. D. Beach; Passaic Metal Ware Company, Passaic, New Jersey; American Art Works Inc.; and Tindeco. American Art Works of Coshocton, Ohio (formerly the Meek Company) printed the greatest number of trays for The Coca-Cola Company, having produced 22 design issues from the years 1910 until 1942. Charles W. Shonk and Passaic Metal Ware Companies each produced early issues for three separate years. The remaining printers produced either one or two tray designs for Coca-Cola.

The vast majority of the serving and tip trays reflect the identity of the lithographer on the lower edge of the picture, where the rim is formed. New collectors should pay close attention to the printer names. Only trays produced for distribution in 1897, 1899, 1920, 1921, 1950, and 1953, as well as the early "topless" art trays, do not have the name of the lithographer printed on them. Many of the trays are actually dated. Still others, such as the 1897 tray, are not dated, but are designated with a date for reference's sake due to the existence of identical matching artwork on a Coca-Cola calendar which is, of course, dated. As a matter of fact, a total of nineteen different trays have used the same artwork as depicted on corresponding advertising calendars issued by Coca-Cola.

The early history of The Coca-Cola Company and the initial development of printing processes and mass merchandising have been covered in this text to provide an interesting historical perspective for the collector of serving trays, or for anyone interested in early antique advertising. Now we will proceed with more specific information related to the years in which Coca-Cola serving trays were issued.

Copyright
A. Dupont

CHAPTER THREE

THE FIRST ISSUES OF COCA-COLA TRAYS, 1897-1910

W e don't know at this point whether any examples of the very first Coca-Cola serving tray exist today. In fact, the circumstances surrounding the issuance of the first tray are shrouded in mystery. As noted previously, *The Black Book/History of Coca-Cola, 1886-1940,* from The Coca-Cola Company archives, contained significant chronological facts regarding firsts in The Coca-Cola Company's use of different concepts/media for advertising. Specific reference is made to use of the "First Coca-Cola advertising tray" in the year 1896. Herein lies the mystery.

The first serving tray known to exist is identified as the "Victorian Girl" tray. This tray is dated as an issue from the year 1897 as a result of its bearing the same artwork as the 1897 Coca-Cola advertising calendar. The notation in the archive's records citing the use of the first serving tray a year earlier, in 1896, could mean two different things. Since the artwork on the Victorian Girl tray is identical to that depicted on the 1897 calendar, it may well have been ordered from the printer in 1896 for issue along with the 1897 calendar. If this were indeed the case, it may well be that the existing tray attributed to the year 1897 is, in fact, the first serving tray issued by The Coca-Cola Company.

On the other hand, was still another tray produced and issued in 1896—one with artwork that was not used elsewhere? If so, it is reasonable to assume that it may well have been an entirely different tray than the one now designated as the 1897 Victorian Girl tray. In this case, no examples of such a tray are presently known to exist. Does one reside in an old trunk somewhere? From time to time, "finds" of early Coca-Cola advertising memorabilia come to the surface. These usually occur by accident, or when the contents of a long-standing family's attic are rummaged through for the first time in decades.

Currently, only a few of the 1897 Victorian Girl trays are known to exist. The very first issues were undoubtedly purchased in quantities of just a few thousand. Further, as is true for all issues of trays in the Company's history, actual quantities of trays purchased for distribution were not documented, and/or the records no longer exist. Considering the

This is one of two portrait photographs used in lithograph advertising by The Coca-Cola Company. It served as the basis for the 1905 serving tray, calendar, and other advertising pieces. Lillian Nordica was a prominent Metropolitan Opera actress and singer of the day.

wear and tear to which these trays were subjected, it is remarkable that any remain today. As with most advertising materials, changes in fashions, product content or design, and the need for ever-more-captivating slogans rendered them quickly out of date. After all, why would a roaring twenties soda fountain owner, who had ready access to attractive new trays featuring contemporary "flapper girls," want to keep those old trays with Victorian Era ladies depicted on them? Instead, it was out with the old and in with the new!

It is reasonable to speculate that Coca-Cola may have been the first company to make use of advertising serving trays. In fact, it is not far-fetched to propose that Coca-Cola may well have had a hand in the conceptual development of the serving tray. A study of the earliest serving trays used for beer, soda, and whiskey advertising suggests this may well be the case. Most, if not all, of the very earliest trays (other than Coca-Cola) date at, or just after, the turn of the century.

The Victorian Girl tray from 1897 is round in shape, lighter in weight than later trays, and measures 9 3/8 inches in diameter. It does not bear the name of the printer. The border design features art which depicts the cola nut and leaf. Similar border art remained a constant on most trays produced until 1910. The actual picture on the tray face depicts a young lady dressed in Victorian attire, sitting at a writing desk and sipping a glass of Coca-Cola. On the writing desk in front of her is a ticket certificate stating, "This card entitles you to one glass of Coca-Cola, free, at the fountain of any dispenser of Coca-Cola." The common themes of "Delicious" and "Refreshing" are also noted off to the side of the picture.

Starting with its first tray in 1897, Coca-Cola began a tradition in choice of art that remained virtually constant over the years. Attractive, young, and wholesome-appearing female models were portrayed in a variety of poses, holding either a glass or a bottle of Coca-Cola, in a scene which included slogans reflecting the most current advertising campaign.

The second known Coca-Cola serving tray is designated as having been issued in 1899, due to the fact that it displayed art matching that on the 1899 Coca-Cola calendar. Depicted on this tray is a popular entertainer of the time known as Hilda Clark. She is shown holding a glass of Coca-Cola, while seated at a writing desk. More will be said later about Hilda Clark and her starring role in Coca-Cola advertising. The colorful 1899 tray is round, 9 5/8 inches in diameter, and includes the slogans "Delicious," "Refreshing," and "Invigorating," along with the Coca-Cola logo. Nearly as rare as the 1897 tray, the 1899 issue is missing in all but a very few of the most prestigious collections of Coca-Cola advertising memorabilia.

Were any trays issued in 1898? If so, were they simply a repeat of the 1897 tray design, or is there still another tray which was used but is, at this point, still unknown? To date, only a handful of the earliest Coca-Cola trays (1897, 1899) are documented and known to exist. Collectors wishing to assemble complete collections that include these ultra-rare trays face a formidable and extremely costly challenge—possibly one that is close to impossible to achieve.

With the turn of the century came dynamic growth in The Coca-Cola Company. Bottle sales were beginning to take off, and two more franchised parent bottlers were approved and licensed. These parent bottlers, in turn, were aggressively setting up local market area bottlers throughout their respective territories. Still, fountain sales remained the backbone of company sales.

In 1900, Coca-Cola issued a regular serving tray, and a matching change tray as well. The serving tray was round, 9 5/8 inches in diameter, and featured a picture of Hilda Clark sitting at a table with a glass of Coca-Cola in one hand. In the other hand she is holding a note stating "Coca-Cola makes flow of thought more easy and reasoning power more vigorous." For the first time, the name of the printer appears on the tray. In this case, the tray was produced by Standard Advertising Company of Coshocton, Ohio. From this date on, most trays carried a printer's notation. Still another first was the availability of a tip or change tray. It displayed the same image of Hilda Clark as the larger 1900 serving tray, but the smaller round change tray was only 5 1/2 inches in diameter. As was the case with the 1899 tray, the 1900 trays also replicated the artwork on the 1900 calendar.

Anthony's Pharmacy, pictured in 1905. This window display indicates how popular Coca-Cola was early in the century. Here, a Pharmacist dedicates an entire window display to Coca-Cola advertising. On the left side of the large Lillian Nordica poster is an oval sign with Hilda Clark art, and on the right, the large oval Hilda Clark tray.

At this point, it is perhaps appropriate to further explore the role and significance of Hilda Clark in early Coca-Cola advertising.

Without a doubt, Hilda Clark reigns as the queen of Coca-Cola advertising for all time! Her likeness was featured on ten serving and change trays, in addition to calendars, signs, cardboard posters, clocks, free drink tickets, bookmarks, trade cards, and a variety of other advertising items. Hilda's likeness was even used on an advertising poster promoting Coca-Cola Chewing Gum. While her tenure lasted just five years (1899 to 1904), the prominence of her image in Coca-Cola advertising was prodigious. Just who was this woman whose image so captured the hearts of Coca-Cola marketers at the turn of the century?

Hilda Clark was an accomplished singer and actress at the time when The Coca-Cola Company was in its infancy. Having made her stage debut in *The Princess Bonnie* in 1895, Miss Clark later established herself as a light opera prima donna in Eastern theaters. Her lovely soprano voice brought her a great deal of notoriety on the stage. Her talents were reviewed in the book *Prima Donnas and Soubrettes*, written by Lewis C. Strang, and published in 1900. Strang wrote of Hilda:

"The divine gift of song has placed Hilda Clark, whose ability as an actress is by no means great, in a position of prominence in the theatrical world. She went on the stage because she could sing, and did not learn to sing because she was on the stage; and, owing to the fact that there is, always has been and always will be a demand for attractive young women with pleasing singing voices, she has had her fair measure of success. Miss Clark has also the added charm of more than ordinary physical attractiveness. She is a blonde of pretty, irregular features. Her personality is winning rather than compelling and her stage presence is good, though there are times when this would have been improved by more

bodily grace than freedom. Byron, who hated a 'dumpy woman,' would have found Miss Clark divinely tall and most divinely fair, but very likely he would have advised to take a mild course in a calisthenics in order to acquire conscious control of a somewhat unruly physique."

There are no known records in existence which detail agreements between Hilda Clark and The Coca-Cola Company, but she obviously had both the appearance and national prominence that Coca-Cola was seeking. Her widespread popularity must have also been recognized as an asset in promoting the up-and-coming beverage. Although Hilda was followed in 1904 by Lillian Nordica, another famous singer featured as a focal point of Coca-Cola advertising, most other subjects chosen for image reproduction on advertising collateral were common models who exemplified the desired features of a pretty face, captivating smile, and wholesome countenance.

For a third straight year, in 1901 The Coca-Cola Company chose the likeness of Hilda Clark for the serving and tip tray issues. The serving tray has beautiful and colorful art depicting Hilda with pink roses and a small oval-shaped picture frame, which reads "Drink Coca-Cola 5¢." The rim design has the familiar Cola nut-and-leaf design used on most trays issued through the 1913 Hamilton King trays. The 1901 serving tray was round, measuring 9 3/4 inches in diameter, while the change tray with the same artwork was 5 5/8 inches in diameter. Both were printed by Meek and Beech Company, Coshocton, Ohio, as imprinted on the tray. Photo copyright credit was also noted on the trays: "From Photo Copyright by Morrison, Chicago, 1900." This simply means that the photographic image itself was copyrighted in 1900, and does not imply that the trays were distributed in that earlier year.

As with other early trays printed using the stone lithography method, the detail, clarity, and subtlety of colors on these trays is simply magnificent. The 1901 issue stands out in this regard with its rich reds, shades of pink, green, and other colors. These trays truly are treasures of beauty and design. The relatively low number of remaining examples provide wonderful displays—lasting testaments to the beauty of early advertising art.

Serving trays were also prominent in The Coca-Cola Company's advertising campaign after the turn of the century. Several publications of the time featured Coca-Cola advertising that portrayed these trays in use in various settings. In the early years, trays were promoted by trade letters to customers. Serving and tip trays were sold to fountain owners for an amount approximating The Coca-Cola Company's cost in purchasing and handling them.

The next issue of serving trays did not occur until 1903. It is likely that the 1901 design was distributed during both 1901 and 1902, and there was, to our current knowledge, no individual and specific tray issued in 1902. Again, the trays issued in 1903 bore the same artwork as the 1903 calendar. Interestingly, 1903 proved to be a year when several varieties of trays were issued. In the change tray category, an issue was done in a round 4 1/8 inches diameter size, with the words "Delicious-Refreshing" on the rim. This very

Above Left: Two ads from the first decade of the 1900s reflect The Coca-Cola Company's earliest print media advertising on a national scale. Both of these ads show metal advertising trays being used for their intended purpose of serving Coca-Cola. Ads like these were seen in The Ladies Home Journal, The Saturday Evening Post *and other publications.*

scarce tip tray does not have a reference to the name of the printer. A larger tip or change tray is 6 inches in diameter, and is marked "Chas. W. Shonk Co., Chicago" to denote the printer. This tip tray has a gold rim without the slogan words.

Also issued in 1903 was a 9 3/4 inches round serving tray with a printer's mark noting "Chas. W. Shonk Co., Chicago," as the printer. In addition to the round Hilda tray in 1903, Coca-Cola issued two versions of a larger oval tray. Both versions of the oval trays are 15 1/8 inches by 18 5/8 inches in size. These were the first of the large-size oval trays produced for The Coca-Cola Company. It is likely that trays of this size were produced to be used as hanging signs as well. The different versions of these large oval trays vary in detail and background color, even though the overall image is the same. Both depict Hilda sitting at a table, holding a glass of Coca-Cola in a silver holder, with an opened letter in front of her. In one version, the letter references six branches of Coca-Cola sales offices. The second version lists seven sales branches. There are also differences in the background colors of the two trays. All of the change and serving trays from 1903 are very scarce and difficult to locate.

Very recently, some previously unknown documents surfaced in the archives of The Coca-Cola Company, and they help shed light on the cost of the early trays. The main document is a purchase order for large 1903 trays and oval signs to be shipped to four Coca-Cola bottlers. The purchase order was issued to the Charles W. Shonk Company, in Chicago. In the same file, shipping documents recorded shipments of trays and signs to the exact bottlers mentioned on The Coca-Cola Company purchase order, and in the same quantities as requested. Undoubtedly, the reference to the large oval tray was the 1903 Hilda Clark tray. The large oval sign was probably the Hilda sign, which was issued with the same artwork as the tray, but with eyelets at the top for hanging it as an actual sign. The cost of the trays was a mere 5.6 cents each! Apparently, the printer inventoried the trays and signs for The Coca-Cola Company. When orders were placed, they were shipped directly from the printer to the designated location.

Until this time, none of the serving or change trays depicted a Coca-Cola bottle on them. With the growing number of bottlers around the country (there were 45 licensed bottlers by 1902), a serving and change tray design was issued which showed a bottle with a diamond-shaped label on its side. The copy on these trays read, "Drink a bottle of carbonated Coca-Cola. The most refreshing drink in the world." To the right of the bottle is a large 5¢ symbol. Although there is no date on either the change tray or the serving tray, it is thought that these were distributed about 1903, and perhaps in later years as well. This tray is far more scarce than the Hilda Clark design of 1903. Very few collectors own this particular tray design in either the serving or change tray versions. Both trays are round, with the serving tray measuring 9 3/4 inches in diameter, while the change tray measures 6 inches in diameter. The name of the printer is designated on the "Bottle" trays as Chas. W. Shonk Co. Litho, Chicago. It is also important to note that a hanging sign was produced with a similar design. This sign is exceedingly rare.

In 1903, The Coca-Cola Company spent $207,000 on advertising and promotion materials. Unfortunately, no records exist which tell us how many serving and change trays were issued each year. It is possible to approximate the numbers issued for some of the

One of the few known documents related to the procurement of serving trays by the Coca-Cola Company, this purchase order was for the Charles S. Shonk Co. of Chicago. It represents orders for trays and metal signs, made in 1903, which cost 5.6 cents each! Corresponding shipping records showing fulfillment of this order were in the same Coca-Cola Company archives file where this document was recently located.

later trays, but not the initial issues. Obviously, the company felt it was gaining a very real merchandising benefit from these beautiful and colorful serving trays. They continued to issue them with different designs for nearly every year from 1900-1910.

There is no record of a new tray being issued in 1904. In all likelihood, the Hilda Clark issues of 1903 were used for both the years 1903 and 1904. The year 1905 witnessed the use of another popular stage star on the serving tray issue. Lillian Nordica, a singer with the Metropolitan Opera Company, was depicted on an oval tray which measured 10 5/8 inches by 12 7/8 inches. The design featured Lillian standing with her arm resting on a table. The familiar coca nut and leaf design is along the rim. There are two versions of this tray. One promotes the purchase of Coca-Cola at soda fountains, and the other touts Coca-Cola in bottles. With the exception of minor differences which depict a bottle on one tray and a glass on the other, the tray art is identical. The company had obviously realized the importance of promoting both fountain and bottle sales. Both versions were printed by "Meek Co. Coshocton, O." and are marked with that inscription. Collectors have dated the tray at 1905 because its artwork is identical to the 1905 calendar issue.

While Lillian Nordica graced the serving tray issues for only one year, her visage appeared on many other advertising pieces. Some of these include menus, posters, calendars, and signs. Confusion has existed over the years as to whether the person depicted was actually Lillian Nordica or Lillian Russell, who was also a contemporary performer. Russell's likeness does appear in advertising for products other than Coca-Cola. However, documentation and original photos exist which establish that the pose used in the advertising artwork featuring Lillian Nordica was done specifically for use by The Coca-Cola Company.

Lillian Norton ("Nordica" was her stage name) was born in 1857 in Farmington, Maine. While a teenager, she displayed singing talent supported by a superb soprano voice. Her talent was of such significance that in the 1870s and 1880s her family sent her to Europe to study music. While overseas, she made her concert and stage debut. Her first major appearance in America was in 1877, when she appeared as a soloist at New York's Madison Square Garden. From there, she toured Europe and achieved acclaim as an accomplished musician.

Having developed her reputation as a singer, a natural extension of Lillian Nordica's talent was to the stage. Following appearances in Europe, she made her American stage debut at the Metropolitan Opera House in 1890, where she portrayed Leonora in "Il Travatore." Nordica continued her career as a singer and actress on the stage through 1913, when she gave a recital in Carnegie Hall. This was perhaps her last major performance—she died shortly thereafter, on May 10, 1914. Groves *Dictionary of Music and Musicians* said of Nordica: "She excelled both in dramatics and singing, but was a better singer than actress."

Like Hilda Clark, Lillian Nordica was chosen as a model for Coca-Cola advertising promotion primarily because of her celebrity status. As time went on, however, the company chose not to use celebrities for most of its artwork. By 1905, their product was already well established throughout the country, so the additional expense of employing celebrities as models was not necessary. The use of celebrities in tray advertising art did not reoccur until the 1930s. Instead, most pictorial artwork featured attractive young ladies adorned in the popular attire of the day.

The next issue of trays is known as the "Juanita" tray. Although undated, its time of issue is considered to be 1906, since the same artwork which graces the tray appears on a Coca-Cola calendar dated 1906. The name "Juanita" has been given to the tray design due to the existence of sheet music for a song entitled "Juanita" which bears the same picture. Typical of tray designs of this era, other items, including a pocket mirror, had the same design.

The actual Juanita tray issues include an oval serving tray which was 10 7/8 inches by 13 inches, and a 4 1/4-inch round change tray. Both have a printer's mark indicating "N. Y. Metal Ceiling Co., N. Y." We know that this printer manufactured just one issue of Coca-Cola trays. We also have some idea of how much The Coca-Cola Company spent for the purchase of these trays. The Secretary's report from The Coca-Cola Company archives recorded purchases of advertising items from various companies. Purchases of $9,457 in 1906, and $8,924 in 1907, were recorded as having been made for the purchase of metal signs from the N. Y. Metal Ceiling Company. Since the next tray issued was printed by the Charles Shonk Co. of Chicago, it is more than likely that the amounts noted as purchases in 1906 and 1907 from the New York firm were indeed for the Juanita serving and change tray design. At a cost of five cents each, 36,762 trays could have been purchased of that design.

In 1906, the company also spent $67,992 on painted wall display advertising; $4,385 on celluloid novelties (pocket mirrors); $56,708 on lithographic printing from Wolf & Company; $5,854 in signs from The Meek Company; and $76,456 with The Massengale Advertising Agency. For all major categories, the company spent $434,907 on advertising—an astronomical amount for the time. Sales agents were exhorted to hang advertising signs in all their territories, and to make sure that Coca-Cola was properly merchandised in soda fountains where it was sold.

About this time, the most intriguing and controversial serving tray was issued. Commonly referred to as the "Topless" tray, it is undoubtedly one of the most beautiful advertising trays ever issued. The art on this round tray shows a beautiful woman, nude to the waist, holding a bottle of Coca-Cola. The rim features a sensational combination of colors and roses. Just as unusual is the tray's advertising, which touts Coca-Cola as an excellent mixer for cocktails. The copy on the tray reads, "Wherever Ginger Ale, Seltzer or Soda is Good, Coca-Cola is better." On the edge of the tray, reference is made to Coca-Cola high balls and Coca-Cola gin rickies. Clearly, this design did not reflect the type of image originally established by The Coca-Cola Company of Atlanta. Instead, it was the doing of one of the parent bottling companies.

The Western Coca-Cola Bottling Company of Chicago, Illinois, was responsible for selection and distribution of the Topless art saloon advertising tray along with several other pieces of risqué advertising related to Coca-Cola promotion. As noted previously, Western Coca-Cola Bottling, along with other regional offices, began operations in 1905 as a wholesale operation to process Coca-Cola syrup orders to local bottlers in designated territories. Western Coca-Cola's territory included several Midwestern and Western states. In part, this helps to explain why an advertising piece like the Topless tray was issued without the blessing of The Coca-Cola Company of Atlanta. Rumor has it that The Coca-Cola Company in Atlanta was incensed that this type of advertising would be associated with Coca-Cola, but nothing concrete exists to substantiate such conjecture. It is known that Asa Candler, a deeply religious man, did not approve of drinking. From the beginning, he sought to promote his product by using advertising graphics which portrayed a distinctly wholesome appearance. Without question, the company would have never approved a risqué advertising piece so obviously designed to adorn the wall of a saloon.

The Topless tray is not dated, but is presumed to have been issued between 1905 and 1908. Supporting evidence suggests that this period is, in fact, when the tray was issued. First, the diamond-shaped paper label shown on the bottle depicted on the tray ceased to be used after 1907. Second, the artwork is consistent with that pictured on beer and whiskey trays of that same time period. Today, the Topless tray is one of the most sought after of all the serving trays. The actual tray is 12 1/4 inches in diameter, lacks a printer's mark, and is designated with the notation of "Western Coca-Cola Bottling Company, Chicago, Illinois" on the bottom edge of the picture. Over the years, most examples of this highly desirable tray have been located in the Midwest and West, where it was originally distributed.

The trays which we now date to the year 1907 are referred to as the "Relieves Fatigue" trays. The picture on this design, which is identical to the one on the 1907 calendar, is of a lovely young lady holding up a glass of Coca-Cola. To the right of her visage is the text "Relieves Fatigue 5¢." Three oval-shaped versions of this tray exist. There is a 10 7/8 inch-by 13 1/4 inches, a 13 3/4 inches by 16 5/8 inches, and a 4 3/8 inches by 6 inches change tray. Many believe this to be among the most outstanding of all of the early Coca-Cola tray designs. All three sizes were printed by the Charles W. Shonk Company, of Chicago.

The beautiful auburn-haired woman in the "Relieves Fatigue" tray is adorned in a lovely green dress. With a purple background and a gold rim, the design is striking, to say the least. Any trays featuring this pictorial design are difficult to locate. The change tray is the most common, but even it can require a lengthy search to find. The medium-sized oval tray is harder to locate, and the large oval tray is very rare. Probably less than fifteen large ovals of this design exist today in collectible condition. Other advertising pieces with the same design as the 1907 tray include a calendar, pocket mirror, self-framed tin sign, and a cardboard sign. The calendar and signs are also exceedingly desirable and rare.

The Coca-Cola Company records document designated purchases of metal supplies totaling $14,197 in 1907, and $24,011 in 1908, for the Charles W. Shonk Company of Chicago, which produced the "Relieves Fatigue" design tray. Undoubtedly, most, if not all, of these funds were allocated to purchases of trays of this design. We have no record of a tray design with the same picture as the 1908 calendar, so it is likely that the "Relieves Fatigue" tray design was also printed and issued in 1908.

In 1909, The Coca-Cola Company issued a new tray design, which has since become known as the "Exhibition Girl" tray. The artwork for this tray was first copyrighted in 1908, and subsequently used again in 1909 on a calendar for that year. In this design, a young woman is seated at a table, holding a glass of Coca-Cola. Behind her is a river with gondolas afloat in the water and illuminated buildings in the background. The rim is blue and gold, with four coca nuts distinctly highlighted. The only slogan on the tray is "Drink Coca-Cola." Three oval versions of this tray include a 13 5/8-inch by 16 5/8-inch tray, a 10 5/8-inch by 13-inch tray, and a 4 1/2-inch by 6 1/4-inch change tray. Collectors refer to the two serving trays as the large and small oval trays. All are marked as printed by "The H. D. Beech Company Coshocton, OH." With this tray design, like its predecessor, the large oval is by far the most difficult of the three sizes to locate, and it must have been produced in much smaller quantities.

Again, we don't know exactly how many of the 1909 design trays were produced, but The Coca-Cola Company Secretary's report notes that $15,586 and $5,783 were spent for metal signs and trays, with those amounts going to the H. D. Beech Co. in the years 1909 and 1910, respectively.

The 1910, Coca-Cola serving trays ushered in several firsts which were to portend things to come. A new rectangular-shaped design was initiated. The tray, issued in a 10 1/2-inch by 13 1/4-inch size, was produced by American Artworks, Coshocton, Ohio. The artwork, copyrighted and dated 1909, depicts a pretty lady wearing a large brim hat with a red rose on it. The slogan on the tray is "Drink Delicious Coca-Cola." In the left hand corner of the tray, the text "The Coca-Cola Girl" is printed. Hamilton King, a noted illustrator of the day, is credited with the art, and his signature is replicated on the tray.

This is the first tray with American Artworks designated as the printer. In this and subsequent years, this firm would go on to produce twenty-two serving tray issues for The Coca-Cola Company. The Coca-Cola Girl artwork on the 1910 tray was also repeated on the 1910 calendar, a postcard, a pocket mirror, and other advertising items.

The 1910 tray design was obviously used in 1911, since no specific 1911 tray is known to exist. The Company Secretary's minutes reflect purchases for metal signs and trays from American Artworks of $8,399 in 1910, and $18,692 in 1911. Based on purchase costs at this period of time, it is plausible to calculate that a minimum of 50,000 change and serving trays were ordered for each of the designs made from 1906 to 1910.

For the serving and advertising tray collector, the formative years of The Coca-Cola Company were prodigious in terms of tray issues and diversity of art. From 1897 until 1910, fifteen serving trays reflecting twelve different designs are known to have been issued. Another nine issues of change trays were distributed. These trays are among the most beautiful and interesting produced over the years. Unfortunately, their survival rate is extremely low, so any of these issues located in excellent and collectible condition are a treasure to prize.

The Coca-Cola Company wanted to promote consistent advertising effort on the part of its bottlers. In April 1909, it published the first issue of *The Coca-Cola Bottler,* which was soon to become a monthly publication. A primary focus of the information in *The Bottler* was on methods and equipment used to productively bottle Coca-Cola. Of equal note was the consistent reference to merchandising. Many issues featured pictures of various county and public fairs and expositions, where local bottlers would display signs, cardboard cutouts, trays, calendars, and other advertising collateral, in addition to selling the famous beverage.

The Company rarely missed the use of public gatherings as an opportunity to merchandise Coca-Cola. At some of these events, serving and change trays were offered to the public as premiums with purchases of Coca-Cola. Calendars were also a major advertising medium, with large quantities being produced for distribution. Route salesmen invariably made sure their territories were decorated with Coca-Cola signs and advertising support items. With advertising expenditures exceeding a million dollars a year, the availability of promotion materials was far from limited.

In 1910, S. C. Dobbs, Sales Manager of the Coca-Cola Company, declared in a quote from *The Coca-Cola Bottler* that "With this company, advertising is no longer looked upon as an expense, but as a splendid dividend producing investment, and the dividend will come just in that proportion the bottlers take advantage of this investment. Two and a half million feet of wall space is working every day inviting the world to drink Coca-Cola".

1897 "VICTORIAN GIRL" ITEMS

Serving Tray
PTO 005.000

1897 "Victorian Girl" Calendar top
PCA 011.000

1897 "Victorian Girl" cardboard Hanging Sign,
6 1/2" x 10 1/2"
PCS 010.000

ITEMS ISSUED BY WESTERN COCA-COLA BOTTLING CO.

The *"Topless" Serving Tray*
PTO 017.000

Folding Trade Card (shown open and closed)
PCT 043.000

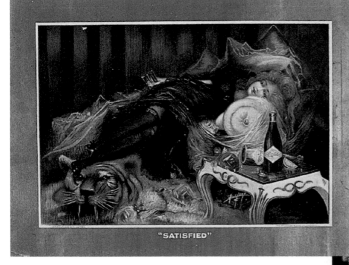

1907 "Satisfied" Paper Sign, 7 1/2" x 10"

C. 1908 "Topless" Vienna Art Plate in original gold, wood frame
PVA 001.000

1903 HILDA CLARK ITEMS

Serving Tray
PTO 011.002

Change Tray
PTT 011.001

Change Tray
PTT 011.002

Serving Tray
PTT 011.002

Paper Sign, 14 3/4" x 19 1/2"
PPS 017.000

1903 Bookmark, 2" x 6"
PBM 010.000

1903 Calendar, 7 3/4" x 15"
PCA 018.001

1905 LILLIAN NORDICA ITEMS

Serving Tray
PTO 014.002

Serving Tray
PTO 014.001

1905 Cardboard Sign, 26" x 46"
PCS 011.000

1905 Calendar,
7 3/4" x 15 1/4"
PCA 020.000

1903 Bookmark, 2 1/4" x
5.25"
PBM 012.000

1905 celluloid-covered
Cardboard Sign, 19" x 25"
PCS 013.000

1905 Magazine Ad with Coupon,
61/2" x 9 3/4"
PCT 052.000

Hanging Sign
PCS 013.000

1910 HAMILTON KING ITEMS

Cardboard Trolley Sign,
11" x 20 1/2"
PCS 016.000

Serving Tray
PTR 019.000

Change Tray
PTT 019.000

Calendar, 8 3/4" x 17 1/2"
PCA 026.000

Matchbook
PSM 015.000

Postcard
PCT 015.000

Pocket Mirror
PMC 009.000

1897 SERVING TRAY
PTO 005.000

The first known (to date) Coca-Cola serving tray. This issue has art identical to that found on the 1897 calendar. Identified by collectors as the "Victorian Girl" tray, only a few examples are known to exist. This round tray is 9 3/8 inches in diameter and is much lighter in weight than trays issued after 1900. No printer's identification or date is noted on the tray. Without a doubt, this is the *piece de resistance* of Coca-Cola advertising memorabilia. As the first known tray issue, it inaugurated a wonderful series of advertising art in the form of the serving tray. A reproduction of this tray design, made in the 1970s, is round, with a 12-inch diameter.

1899 SERVING TRAY
PTO 007.000

The second known serving tray featured the visage of the famous singer and actress, Hilda Clark. The tray is dated 1899 due to its having the same art as two calendars dated 1899. Only a few examples of this tray have been located. This round tray is 9 5/8 inches in diameter, and shares the lightweight characteristic of the 1897 tray. The use of Hilda Clark on this tray marked the beginning of a theme which resulted in her image being used on ten serving and change trays, in addition to many other advertising pieces.

1900 SERVING TRAY
PTO 008.000

The 1900 tray featured Hilda Clark drinking a glass of Coca-Cola with the "Delicious, Refreshing" slogan that helped make Coca-Cola the most famous soft drink in the world. This round tray is 9 5/8 inches in diameter and, for the first time, the name of the printer is reflected on the center bottom edge of the picture as "Standard Advertising Co., Coshocton, O." From this point on, the vast majority of the trays indicated the name of the printer.

The weight of the tray is heavier than the 1897 and 1899 issues, and is typical of the trays produced by manufacturers after 1900. The first known change tray was also produced using this same design. As with the previous issues, this is a very rare tray. The same art was used on two different calendars. A reproduction of this tray was made in the 1970s, which does not note the name of the printer.

1900 CHANGE TRAY
PTT 008.000

With artwork depicting Hilda Clark which was identical to the 1900 serving tray, this was the first change tray known to have been produced for the Coca-Cola Company. Issued in a round shape with a 5 1/2-inch diameter, the name of the printer appears on the center bottom edge of the picture as "Standard Advertising Co., Coshocton, O." In addition to the serving tray, two calendars were also produced using the same artwork.

1901 SERVING TRAY
PTO 009.000

This beautiful tray depicted still another visage of Hilda Clark. With a more interesting and detailed picture than the first trays, the price of a Coca-Cola at 5¢ is reflected on a tray for the first time. Produced in a round shape with a diameter of 9 3/4 inches, the name of the printer (Meek and Beech Company, Coshocton, Ohio) is designated on the tray in the red border in the center, below the picture. Also printed on the tray in the lower center area of the picture is the notation "From photo copyright by Morrison, Chicago, 1900." Although the art was copyrighted in 1900, the tray is believed to have been distributed in 1901, along with a calendar dated that same year with artwork identical to the tray. A change tray, bookmark, glass change receiver, and a paper sign were also produced using the same artwork.

1901 CHANGE TRAY
PTT 009.000

With artwork identical to the serving tray issued in the same year, this colorful piece was produced in a 5 5/8-inch diameter round size. Marked in the lower center edge of the picture as having been printed by "Meek and Beech Company, Coshocton, O.," it depicts Hilda Clark and the slogan "Delicious and Refreshing," which was widely used by the Coca-Cola Company for many years. There is another slightly different variation of this change tray with a rim that protrudes higher from the flat portion of the tray. This same art was used on the 1901 calendar, a glass change receiver, and a paper sign, as well.

1901 CHANGE TRAY (VARIATION)
PTT 009.001

With artwork identical to the serving tray issued in the same year, this colorful piece was produced in a 5 5/8-inch diameter round size. Marked in the lower center edge of the picture as having been printed by "Meek and Beech Company, Coshocton, O.," it depicts Hilda Clark and the slogan "Delicious and Refreshing," which was widely used by the Coca-Cola Company for many years. This is the variation of this change tray with a rim that protrudes higher from the flat portion of the tray. This same art was used on the 1901 calendar, a glass change receiver, and a paper sign, as well.

1903 SERVING TRAY
(ROUND VERSION)
PTO 011.002

In 1903, there were actually three serving tray variations of the same artwork which again featured Hilda Clark. The round tray is properly referred to as the 1903 Hilda, and was produced in a 9 3/4-inch diameter size. The name of the printer is reflected on the center bottom edge of the picture as "Chas. W. Shonk Co., Chicago". The tray also reflects the "Delicious, Refreshing" slogan which was so prevalent in early Coca-Cola advertising. Variations of nearly identical artwork were used on two different-sized change trays and two large oval trays. As with earlier trays, this issue is dated based on the fact that a calendar was distributed with nearly identical artwork for the year 1903.

1903 CHANGE TRAY
(SMALL ROUND VARIETY)
PTT 011.002

Two issues of change trays were produced in the 1903 series of trays. The first was made in a 4 1/8-inch diameter round size. With the words "Delicious" on the top and "Refreshing" on the bottom of the tray, it does not bear the inscription of the printer.

The artwork matches the pose of Hilda Clark found on all of the 1903 serving and change trays, but the envelope and letter depicted on the larger trays is not present on this small issue.

1903 CHANGE TRAY
(LARGER ROUND VARIETY)
PTT 011.001

The other 1903 change tray issue presented artwork more similar to that of the serving trays issued in 1903 than the small round variety. Produced in a 6-inch round diameter size, the name of the printer is listed on the center bottom edge of the picture as "Chas. W. Shonk Co., Chicago."

1903 SERVING TRAY
(LARGE OVAL SIZE)
PTO 011.001

Known today as "Big Hilda" (Hilda Clark) by collectors, this tray's artwork is nearly identical to the 1903 round tray, but this tray is much larger. With an abundance of purples and bright golds, this tray is a stunning sight in its imposing 15 1/8-inch by 18 5/8-inch oval size. As with the round version, it was printed by the "Chas. W Shonk Co., Chicago" as seen on the center of the bottom edge of the picture. Another similar, but even more rare,

variant of this tray exists (not pictured). It is differentiated by darker purples and golds, and the note on the table refers to only six Coca-Cola sales offices, while the brighter, more attractive variation lists seven. An oval sign with artwork identical to this tray was also produced—it is rare and highly prized. All in all, three serving tray versions, two change trays, an oval sign, and the 1903 calendar were produced in this time period with the same Hilda Clark pose.

THE BOTTLE SERVING TRAY (Ca. 1903)
PTO 012.000

This unusual tray featured only a bottle as artwork. It was distributed around 1903, or perhaps a couple of years after that. Bottling operations were becoming widespread at this point, so promotion of Coca-Cola in bottles made good sense. The tray was issued in a 9 3/4-inch round size, but did not bear the mark of a printer. A nearly identical design is found on a 6-inch round change tray. Also interesting is the use of copy, which extolled Coca-Cola as "The most refreshing drink in the world." This slo-gan signaled The Coca-Cola Company's interest in international markets. Two other signs were produced with similar artwork featuring the bottle. One was a round, 6-inch sign, with eyelets for hanging stamped into the top rim. The other is an 8 1/2-inch by 10 1/2-inch oval sign featuring an identical bottle design, but with some variations in the artwork surrounding the bottle. These trays are extremely rare, and rank among the most difficult early issues to locate.

THE BOTTLE CHANGE TRAY (Ca. 1903)
PTT 012.000

With artwork and slogans identical to that of the larger serving tray, this change tray was issued in a round, 6-inch size. As with the serving tray, it is exceedingly rare. There is no indication of the printer of this tray or the serving tray, although a 6-inch hanging sign was produced with artwork nearly identical to that of the change and serving tray which indicates "Chas. W Shonk Co., Chicago" as the printer. It is, therefore, likely that the Bottle artwork serving and change trays were printed by this same firm.

1905 SERVING TRAYS
PTO 014.001   PTO 014.002

Opera singer, Lillian Nordica, was featured on this tray. Collectors refer to it as the "Lillian Nordica," or simply the "Nordica" tray. Although very similar in overall appearance, there are two variations of this tray. The main difference is that one features a bottle of Coca-Cola on the table next to Lillian Nordica, while the other depicts a glass. The bottle versions also used copy which stated "Drink Carbonated Coca-Cola in bottles" while the other stated "Drink Coca-Cola at soda fountains." Both trays are marked

"Meek Co., Coshocton, Ohio" on the lower edge of the picture and are 10 5/8 inches by 12 7/8 inches in size. A calendar dated 1905, a large cardboard sign, celluloid sign, small oval sign, bookmark, and a menu were also produced with this artwork. Unlike the serving trays distributed from 1900 to 1903, no matching change trays are known to exist. Reproductions of this artwork were done on rectangular trays produced in the 1970s.

1906 SERVING TRAY
PTO 015.000

Known by collectors today as the "Juanita" tray, this issue used the same artwork as the cover of a piece of sheet music to a song entitled "Juanita." Oval in shape, the tray measures 10 7/8 inches by 13 inches, and references the source of the artwork with the statement "From Painting copyright 1906 by Wolf and Co. Phila. PA." which is printed on the lower left-hand side of the picture.

The name of the printer is given on the lower right-hand edge of the picture as "N. Y. Metal Ceiling Co., N.Y." A change tray was also produced with the same artwork as the serving tray. Identical artwork was also featured on the 1906 calendar, a pocket mirror, and several pieces of sheet music.

1906 CHANGE TRAY
PTT 015.000

Produced with the same image of "Juanita" as the serving tray, the change tray was issued in a 4 1/4-inch diameter round size. Two notations are included on the tray. The first, located on the lower right edge of the picture, shows the printer as "N. Y. Metal Ceiling Co., N.Y." The second documents the source of the artwork as "From Painting copyright 1906 by Wolf and Co. Phila. PA." This inscription is located on the picture's lower left edge.

1907 SERVING TRAY
(MEDIUM OVAL)
PTO 016.001

This has become known as the "Relieves Fatigue" tray due to the use of the early "Relieves Fatigue" advertising slogan on the tray. Produced in three oval-shaped sizes (which included a change tray, medium oval tray, and large oval tray), the design features a rich array of gold, green, and purple, and other colors which highlight a lovely, young model holding a glass of Coca-Cola. The medium-sized serving tray measures 10 7/8 inches by 13 1/4 inches, and is marked on the lower edge of the picture as having been printed by "Chas. W. Shonk Co., Litho, Chicago." This same artwork was used on a calendar dated 1907, a pocket mirror, and a rare, self-framed tin sign issued during this same time period.

1907 SERVING TRAY
(LARGER OVAL)
PTO 016.002

A second version of the "Relieves Fatigue" tray, this issue was produced in a 13 3/4-inch by 16 5/8-inch size which shows more of the picture than the smaller oval tray. It is marked on the lower edge of the picture as having been printed by "Chas. W. Shonk Co., Litho, Chicago." Obviously, very few of these large trays were produced—few are known to exist in any state of preservation. In addition to its use on the medium oval and large oval serving trays, the same artwork was used on a change tray, a calendar dated 1907, a pocket mirror, and a rare, self-framed tin sign issued during this same time period.

1907 CHANGE TRAY
PTT 016.000

The "Relieves Fatigue" change tray for 1907 contains artwork identical to that on the large oval serving tray. Produced in a 4 3/8-inch by 6-inch oval size, the printer is noted on the tray, in the lower edge of the picture, as "Chas. W. Shonk Co., Litho, Chicago." In addition to use on the change tray and the two oval serving trays, this same artwork appeared on a calendar dated 1907, a pocket mirror, and a rare, self-framed tin sign issued during this same time period.

Wherever Ginger Ale, Seltzer or Soda is Good

DRINK "Coca-Cola" "HIGH BALLS"

DRINK Coca-Cola "GIN RICKIES"

Coca-Cola is Better - Try It.

WESTERN COCA-COLA BOTTLING CO., CHICAGO, ILL.

DRINK Coca-Cola

THE "TOPLESS" SERVING TRAY (1905-07)
PTO 017.000

Produced and distributed sometime between 1905-1907, this is the most controversial tray ever issued to promote Coca-Cola. Distributed by The Coca-Cola Bottling Company of Chicago, the artwork and label design on the bottle point to this period of time. With its risqué artwork, the term "Topless" has become the designated reference word for this tray for obvious reasons. Designed to promote Coca-Cola as a mixer for cocktails, the piece was produced for use in saloons. Round in shape, the tray is 12 1/4 inches in diameter, and does not contain an inscription giving the name of the printer. The only marking on the tray referring to its origination is located on the bottom center edge of the picture, where it states "Western Coca-Cola Bottling Co., Chicago, ILL." The Western Coca-Cola Bottling Company did distribute a Vienna Art Plate with the same artwork as the topless tray, but it did not have any advertising on its face. Beyond that, the artwork was not used to promote Coca-Cola in any other formats, and it was not a part of the advertising program developed or approved by The Coca-Cola Company in Atlanta.

1909 SERVING TRAY
(MEDIUM OVAL)
PTO 018.001

Produced from artwork copyrighted in 1908, this design has become referred to as the "Exhibition Girl" tray. As with the 1907 tray art, the Exhibition Girl tray was produced in three formats, including a change tray, medium oval, and large oval size tray. The medium oval serving tray was produced in a 10 5/8-inch by 13-inch size. A printer's inscription is located in the lower edge of the picture which reads: "The H. D. Beech Co., Coshocton, Oh." The same artwork was used on a pocket mirror and a calendar dated 1909.

1909 SERVING TRAY
(LARGE OVAL)
PTO 018.002

With artwork identical to the medium oval "Exhibition Girl" tray, this large oval version measures 13 5/8 inches by 16 5/8 inches, and is much more difficult to locate than the medium oval tray. The printer's inscription on this tray is also located on the lower edge of the picture, and reads, "The H. D. Beech Co, Coshocton, Oh." In addition to use of this same artwork on the medium oval serving tray and change tray, it was used on a pocket mirror and a calendar dated 1909.

1909 CHANGE TRAY
PTT 018.000

The "Exhibition Girl" artwork present on the 1909 change tray matched that of the medium and large oval serving trays. Issued in a 4 1/2-inch by 6 1/4-inch oval size, the printer's inscription, located on the lower edge of the picture, reads, "The H. D. Beech Co., Coshocton, Oh." In addition to the use of this same artwork on the medium oval and large oval serving tray, it was used on a calendar dated 1909, and on a pocket mirror.

1910 SERVING TRAY
PTR 019.000

This tray issue marked the first design produced in a rectangular format. Produced from artwork copyrighted in a 1909 painting by Hamilton King, the tray is titled "The Coca-Cola Girl." The printer's designation is reflected on the lower right-hand edge of the picture where it states, "The American Artworks, Coshocton, Ohio." In the left-hand corner of the picture is an inscription reading, "Painting only copyrighted by the Coca-Cola Company 1909." The size of the tray is 10 1/2 inches by 13 1/4 inches. This was the first tray issue produced by American Artworks. An oval change tray was also issued with the same artwork. In addition, the design was used on the 1910 calendar, postcard, pocket mirror, and other advertising items. A reproduction of the 1910 tray produced in the 1970s does not include the name of the printer or the trademark notation in the tail of the large "C" in the words Coca-Cola.

1910 CHANGE TRAY

PTT 019.000

With the same Hamilton King artwork as found on the 1910 rectangular serving tray, this change tray was issued in a 4 3/8-inch by 6 1/8-inch oval size. It bears the title of the copyrighted artwork of "The Coca-Cola Girl" in the center of the lower edge of the pic-ture. As with the serving tray, it was printed by "The American Artworks, Coshocton, Ohio." In addition to use on the serving and change trays, the design was used on the 1910 calendar, as well as on a postcard, pocket mirror, and other advertising items.

ICE COLD

Coca-Cola

TRADE MARK
REGISTERED

SOLD HERE

Ca. 1914 tin embossed sign, 19" by 27", featuring the paper label bottle used during this time period. Tin signs, as well as serving trays, are prized collector items from the 1911 to 1919 period when only a few different examples were produced.

CHAPTER FOUR

TRAY ISSUES OF THE YEARS, 1911-1919

The years from 1910 to 1920 were not terribly prolific in terms of the variety of trays issued. After the first Hamilton King artwork tray of "The Coca-Cola Girl" in 1910 and 1911 was produced, it was not until 1913 that a new tray design was offered. This issue also utilized the art of Hamilton King, depicting a beautiful young lady wearing a large hat and holding a fluted glass of Coca-Cola which had "5¢" etched on it. The advertising copy stated "Drink Coca-Cola; Delicious and Refreshing." For the first time, a tray was issued in both the new rectangular shape and the traditional oval shape. A change tray with the same art completed the available selection of trays.

The 1913 trays were all printed by "Passaic Metalware Co., Passaic, New Jersey," and are marked as such. Hamilton King's name is also noted as the artist holding copyright to the portrait of the young lady. The complete artwork is also noted as copyrighted by Wolf and Company, in 1912. The sizes of the trays are 10 1/4 inches by 13 1/4 inches (rectangular), 12 1/2 inches by 15 1/4 inches (oval), and 4 3/8 inches by 6 1/8 inches (change tray). The same artwork was also used for the 1913 calendar and for a festoon window display.

This was likely the first year in which truly significant quantities of trays were produced and released. Notes from the advertising account section of The Coca-Cola Company Secretary's notes reflect purchases from Wolf and Company of $66,216 in 1912, and of $37,299 in 1913. The same document shows additional purchases of items from Passaic Metal Ware Co. in 1913 of $42,371. In all likelihood, these expenditures were related to tray purchases. As is noted earlier, company documents show that two million serving trays (this number undoubtedly included change trays) were distributed by The Coca-Cola Company in 1913. Today's collector must find this number to be astounding, since it is difficult to find 1913 Coca-Cola serving trays in excellent condition.

Change and growth was the norm for The Coca-Cola Company even during the teens. By 1912, the number of franchised bottlers in the United States had risen to 691. Coca-Cola was available internationally in many countries, such as Japan, New Zealand, China, France, and Holland, to mention just a few. In the course of its first twenty-five years, Coca-Cola had become a worldwide beverage.

Trays issued in 1914 were produced in the same sizes and shapes as the 1913 trays, and have become known as the "Betty" trays. The designation is derived from the fact that beneath the picture on the 1914 calendar appears the title "Betty," and although the tray is not so marked, the pretty young woman on the tray is identical to the one on the calendar. A self-framed tin sign, poster, and other advertising collateral were produced with the same "Betty" artwork. The tray was issued in three sizes, including a 10 5/8-inch by 13 3/8-inch rectangular tray, a 12 3/8-inch by 15 1/2-inch oval serving tray, and a 4 3/8-inch by 6 1/2-inch change tray. The picture portrays a young woman in a pink and white laced dress, and wearing a fancy bonnet with a dark green background. "Passaic Metalware Co. Litho, of Passaic, New Jersey" is printed on all three examples. Of note to collectors: This was the last Coca-Cola serving tray printed using the old stone lithography process.

As with the rectangular 1913 issue, the oval Betty tray design is one of several which was later reproduced in the 1970s. There are various ways to distinguish the reproduction from an original. One way is to compare the printing color and depth of each example. The original, printed using the old stone lithography process, displays much deeper and more subtle colors in side-by-side comparison with the newer reproduction, which was printed with more modern processes. Other distinguishing characteristics include the existence of the printer's name on originals, and placement of the trademark symbol.

The "Betty" tray was widely used by Coca-Cola for several years as a promotion item, and was undoubtedly printed in large quantities. We don't know the exact number of trays issued with the Betty art, but we do know that 10,000 of the larger self-framed tin signs with this art were distributed. Much less expensive to produce than the large sign, it's likely that a couple million Betty trays may have been produced. Today's collector could only dream of taking a ride in a time machine back to the Rockland, Maine, Pure Food show held in 1917. A picture from the April 1917 issue of *The Coca-Cola Bottler* shows how the local Coca-Cola bottler had a display booth at the show that included tin signs, calendars, cardboard cutouts, an Ingraham advertising clock, and a "Betty" tray, prominently displayed. Bottlers were encouraged to aggressively promote Coca-Cola by using available advertising materials to provide maximum exposure at every possible opportunity. Similarly, soda fountain owners were encouraged to fill their window displays with trays and other advertising materials.

The only other tray design issued in the teens was first produced in 1916, with artwork identical to that displayed on the calendar for that same year. Today, this tray is known by collectors, and erroneously so, as the "Elaine" tray. Over the years, collectors have nicknamed many of the trays. In the case of the 1914 "Betty" tray, the designation is both correct and appropriate, since the calendar with matching art has the title "Betty" noted below the picture. Most other tray and calendar artwork was not titled, and name designations have simply been invented to allow for identification of various trays. Many of these names will be used in this book. However, this will not be the case when we refer to the 1916 tray.

In 1915, Coca-Cola issued a calendar entitled "Elaine." Clearly, though, the 1915 artwork is not the same as either the 1916 tray or the 1916 calendar. The actual artwork for the 1916 tray is copyrighted as "Girl with a Basket of Flowers," and

The Rockland, Maine, Pure Food Show in 1917 featured a booth sponsored by the Rockland Bottler who displayed a wide array of Coca-Cola advertising art. Included are the "Betty" tray, two calendars, cardboard cutouts, tin signs, a celluloid sign, and a Coca-Cola advertising clock.

shows an attractive young woman sitting on a wicker table, holding a glass of Coca-Cola in her left hand. The "Elaine" designation for this tray is, therefore, incorrect, since the tray should be known by the title of the actual copyrighted artwork. A very colorful design, this marked the first year that modern photo-lithography was used to produce a Coca-Cola tray.

Also, for the first time, a new and short-lived tray size and shape was used. The 1916 tray was produced in a rectangular size 8 1/2 inches wide by 19 inches long. No one knows just why this new size was selected. The obvious difficulty of balancing soft drinks on this narrow tray design must have been its downfall, as this size was never used again. An oval change tray measuring 4 3/8 inches by 6 1/8 inches was also offered along with the larger tray. Both were printed by Stelad Signs Passaic Metalware Co., Passaic, NJ, and are marked as such on the left-hand corner edge of the actual picture. This same design was also used on a pocket mirror, cardboard sign, self-framed tin sign, and a few other items, in addition to the 1916 calendar.

No other trays were issued in the teens. World War I was in full swing by 1917, and metal shortages made production of anything other than armaments and war materials unpatriotic. While Coca-Cola may have ordered reprints of the 1914 and 1916 trays, they were not interested in issuing any new designs, undoubtedly due to the war effort. And, other important events that would help shape the company's future were occurring with some regularity.

The original Coca-Cola Bottle contained 8 ounces of soda. This changed to the shapely 6 1/2 ounce size in the now-famous "hobble skirt" bottle, patented in 1915. This design was named after the hobble skirts worn by ladies of the day. The renowned Coca-Cola bottle design was a packaging innovation which further distinguished the Coca-Cola product. Approved by bottlers in 1916 as the chosen design for future bottling of Coca-Cola, history had again been made.

By 1917, syrup sales exceeded ten million gallons for the first time. Although there had been several challenges to the Coca-Cola trademark by opportunists hoping to capture a share of the marketing genius with which The Coca-Cola Company had so brilliantly succeeded, the Company persevered. In 1919, a major court ruling protected the copyright of the Coca-Cola trade name. This helped solidify the base for dynamic future growth by legally warding off would-be imitators. Against this backdrop, in 1919, Asa Candler sold the company for $25,000,000 to Ernest Woodruff and an investment group. Shortly thereafter, the company was incorporated in Delaware as a publicly held firm, and stock was offered and publicly traded.

This colorful piece shows the artist painting the girl featured on the 1916 tray. This particular image refers to "One of America's famous artists painting the 1916 calendar girl."

1913 SERVING TRAY
(RECTANGULAR)
PTR 024.000

As with some of the earlier tray issues, three formats were used for the 1913 tray. A large oval size tray, a rectangular tray, and an oval change tray. On each, the art of Hamilton King was featured, and is noted on the tray as "Copyright 1912 Wolf & Co." As such, over the years, collectors have dubbed this the "Hamilton King Girl" tray. All three trays have inscriptions noting the printer, as well. The printer is noted on the bottom edge of the tray as "Passaic Metalware Co., Passaic, New Jersey." The rectangular tray is 10 1/2 inches by 13 1/4 inches. In addition to the other trays with this design, the same artwork was used on a 1913 calendar and a cardboard cutout. A reproduction of the 1913 rectangular tray produced in the 1970s does not include the name of the printer or the trademark notation in the tail of the large "C" in the words Coca-Cola.

1913 SERVING TRAY
(LARGE OVAL)
PTO 024.000

The large oval version of the 1913 "Hamilton King Girl" tray was produced in a 12 1/2-inch by 15 1/4-inch format. As with the other trays, the printer is noted on the bottom edge of the tray as "Passaic Metalware Co., Passaic, New Jersey." The tray is also marked "Copyright 1912 Wolf & Co."— consistent with the other trays with this same artwork. In addition to the other trays with this design, the same artwork was used on a 1913 calendar, as well as on a cardboard cutout.

1913 CHANGE TRAY
PTT 024.000

Displaying the "Hamilton King Girl" artwork of the 1913 rectangular and oval serving trays, these were issued in a 4 3/8-inch by 6 1/8-inch oval size. This change tray design has the same markings as those on the serving trays, which include the printer's inscription on the bottom edge of the tray as "Passaic Metalware Co., Passaic, New Jersey." The tray is also marked "Copyright 1912 Wolf & Co." The same artwork was used on a 1913 calendar and a cardboard cutout, as well as other trays.

1914 SERVING TRAY
(RECTANGULAR)
PTR 025.000

Named the "Betty" tray due to matching calendar artwork with that name designation on it, this tray is a favorite among collectors. Produced in three formats, including a change tray, rectangular tray, and large oval tray, all were printed by the "Passaic Metalware Co., litho. Passaic, New Jersey" and are so marked in the corner edge of the picture. The rectangular issue above was produced in a 10 5/8-inch by 13 3/8-inch size. The "Betty" art was very popular, and, as a result, was used on a large, self-framed tin sign, the 1914 calendar, posters, and in print media advertising. As with the other 1914 tray issues, this would prove to be the last of the trays printed using the "stone lithography" process. All three trays have "The Coca-Cola Company" notation on them.

1914 SERVING TRAY
(LARGE OVAL)
PTO 025.000

With artwork identical to the 1914 calendar, change tray, and rectangular "Betty" tray, the large oval version was produced in a 12 3/8-inch by 15 1/2-inch size. Printed by the "Passaic Metalware Co., litho. Passaic, New Jersey," the tray is so marked in the left corner edge of the picture. A reproduction of this tray (the oval version) was issued by The Coca-Cola Company, but there are some clear-cut ways to identify the original from the copy. The reproduction, produced in the 1970s, does not include the name of the printer or the trademark notation in the tail of the large "C" in the words Coca-Cola. The Betty art was also used on a self-framed tin sign, the 1914 calendar, posters, and in print media advertising.

1914 CHANGE TRAY
PTT 025.000

Displaying artwork identical to that found on the large oval 1914 "Betty" tray, this change tray was issued in a 4 3/8-inch by 6 1/2-inch oval size. The printer's inscription is found on the lower left edge of the picture, and is noted as "Passaic Metalware Co., litho. Passaic, New Jersey." A reproduction of this change tray pro- duced in the 1970s does not include the name of the printer or the trademark notation in the tail of the large "C" in the words Coca-Cola. In addition to use on the 1914 serving and change trays, the Betty art was also used on a self-framed tin sign, the 1914 calendar, posters, and in print media advertising.

1916 SERVING TRAY
PTR 026.000

Collectors often refer to this as the "Elaine" tray, but the correct designation of the art is the "Girl with a Basket of Flowers," which is the actual copyrighted artwork matching that found on the tray. What is truly unique to this tray is its size and shape. Unlike any other tray produced, this version was formatted in a long 8 1/2-inch by 19-inch rectangular size. This odd size obviously never found favor since it was never produced again. An oval change tray was also produced with the same artwork. Both the serving and change trays bear an inscription of the printer's name in the left-hand corner of the picture which reads "Stelad Signs Passaic Metalware Co, Passaic, NJ." The artwork was also used on the 1917 calendar, a self-framed tin sign, a pocket mirror, and other advertising items. A reproduction of this tray, produced in the 1970s, does not include the name of the printer or the trademark notation in the tail of the large "C" in the words Coca-Cola.

1916 CHANGE TRAY
PTT 026.000

With the same "Girl with a Basket of Flowers" artwork as the 1916 long rectangular tray, this piece was issued in a 4 3/8-inch by 6 1/8-inch oval size. As with the serving tray, the change tray bears an inscription of the printer's name in the left-hand corner of the picture reading, "Stelad Signs Passaic Metalware Co, Passaic, NJ." Both this and the "Betty" change trays were obviously made in large quantities—they are the least difficult of the original change trays to locate today. In addition to the change and serving tray, the artwork was also used on the 1917 calendar, a self-framed tin sign, a pocket mirror, and other advertising items. A reproduction of this change tray, produced in the 1970s, does not include the name of the printer or the trademark notation in the tail of the large "C" in the words Coca-Cola.

CHAPTER FIVE

TRAY ISSUES OF THE 1920s

By 1920, the war was over and the metal shortage had ended as well. The production of serving trays began again. The Company's annual expenditures for advertising for 1920 were in excess of 2.3 million dollars. Consistent with the look of trays from the earlier years, the 1920 tray artwork pictured an attractive young woman identical to that used on the calendar for the same year.

Because the 1920 tray depicts a pretty young lady holding a glass of Coca-Cola, with a golf scene behind her, collectors have named this the "Golfing Girl" tray. Similar to the 1913 and 1914 tray production, three sizes of this tray were issued. The largest tray was an oval measuring 13 3/4 inches by 16 3/4 inches. A rectangular tray was issued in a 10 1/2-inch by 13 1/4-inch size. And there was also a change tray in a 4 1/2-inch by 16 3/4-inch oval shape. From this point on, all future trays would be issued in the rectangular size of 10 1/2 inches by 13 1/4 inches. This would prove to be the last year for production of large-size oval and change trays. Unlike most issues, the 1920 trays did not bear a printer's mark.

In 1920, the first official Bottlers Advertising List was produced. This list reflected what bottlers had to pay for various advertising items. Shortly thereafter, the Company also offered a cooperative advertising program. Under the terms of this program, Coca-Cola would allow any credit due for a previous year's syrup purchases to count toward defraying the cost of advertising materials. On the 1920 advertising list, oblong trays were offered to bottlers for 22¢ each, and a small change tray was available for 4¢ each.

Beginning with the 1920 trays, The Coca-Cola Company issued at least one tray for each following year until 1942. The second tray issued in the 1920s is commonly referred to as the "Autumn Girl" tray. Still others refer to the tray as the "Navy Girl" tray, since the young lady seen holding a glass of Coca-Cola is attired in a blue hat resembling a stylish Navy hat. As noted previously, collectors have made-up names for the various trays issued over the years. Few of the names are actually based on titles of original artwork, since most of the oils and illustrations have been lost or destroyed, and records regarding this type of information no longer exist.

Tray art was often used on many other pieces, in addition to calendars. This example of a lovely cardboard cutout sign adorned the windows of many soda fountains during the mid-twenties, though only a handful exist today. The picture matches that of the 1924 tray.

Like the 1920 tray design, the 1921 "Autumn Girl" or "Navy Girl" tray is one of the few that doesn't have the name of the printer noted anywhere on it. It is dated for reference's sake as a 1921 issue because it features the same artwork as the 1921 calendar. Some collectors of Coca-Cola advertising memorabilia enjoy selecting a favorite tray design from a given year, and displaying all of the related items with that same artwork. In the case of the 1921 tray art, the calendar for the same year provides a nice display positioned next to the tray.

The 1922 tray issue is customarily referred to by collectors as the "Summer Girl" tray. Dated 1921, and marked as being printed by "H.D. Beech Co., Coshocton O.," this tray was actually made for issue in 1922, along with a calendar for that same year that displays matching artwork. The calendar is a favorite of collectors because it shows not only the girl pictured on the tray, but also a baseball game scene. The tray design is unique among Coca-Cola tray art in that it has little square gold dots along the rim surrounding the picture. This issue has always been a favorite among collectors and, as with many of the trays, it is quite a challenge to find one in original-quality condition.

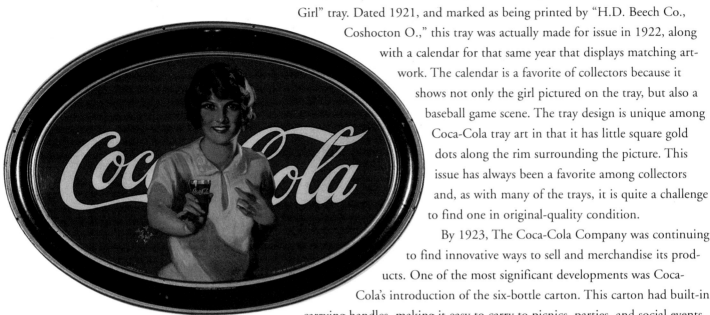

By 1923, The Coca-Cola Company was continuing to find innovative ways to sell and merchandise its products. One of the most significant developments was Coca-Cola's introduction of the six-bottle carton. This carton had built-in carrying handles, making it easy to carry to picnics, parties, and social events of all kinds. The company actually hired employees to go door-to-door to sell Coca-Cola in the new carton. Armed with bottle openers which they were happy to install in people's homes, these door-to-door sales representatives proved to be very effective in the effort to increase sales. The new carton, combined with aggressive new sales approaches, helped to create the important home consumption market for Coca-Cola. Robert Woodruff's desire to make Coca-Cola available everywhere was being realized. With convenient cartons now available for the consumer, the company had significantly expanded its potential marketplace.

1926 tin embossed oval sign, 13" by 19". This art was not used on a serving tray, but on a number of different tin signs. Each sign was produced in two variations with the model holding either a glass or a bottle.

Serving trays were available to bottlers and the fountain trade in 1923 for $137.50 per thousand, or .13 3/4¢ each. Calendars that year were priced at $45.00 per thousand, and large metal signs went for $157.00 per thousand. These figures are unimaginable to today's collectors who pay hundreds of dollars each for the precious few remaining examples of Coca-Cola merchandising.

In 1923, The Coca-Cola Company issued a new tray, which was merely a variation on a long-standing theme. An attractive lady, attired in a lovely evening dress and coat, is shown holding a Coca-Cola glass. This issue also matches the art displayed on the 1923 calendar, and the tray is dated that same year. As with most of the serving trays produced from 1923 until 1942, the printer was "American Artworks, Coshocton, Ohio," and this information is noted on the bottom edge of the picture. Collectors need to be aware of this all-important printer's designation. A reproduction of this tray was made by The Coca-Cola Company in the 1970s. Care was taken at that time to avoid placing the original printer's name on the reproduction tray. Additionally, the reproduction tray does not contain the Coca-Cola trademark in the

tail of the "C" of the word "Coca," as it is on the original. Colors and details on reproduction trays are not as
crisp and sharp, either. A separate section of this book
deals with reproduction trays and how to distinguish
them from originals.

With the overwhelming growth of bottle sales,
The Coca-Cola Company recognized that it needed to
continue its aggressive approach to fountain sales. In
January 1924, the first issue of *The Red Barrel* was
released. This publication was aimed at increasing
syrup sales by providing a reference to the merchandising of Coca-Cola in soda fountains, department
stores, and other similar locations where the drink
was served from a fountain dispenser. The early
issues of the publication offer insights into the brilliant merchandising of Coca-Cola. Pictures of outstanding fountain displays with signs, trays, clocks, calendars, and a plethora of advertising material are featured
in many issues. The serving tray continued, as in the beginning, to be an integral part of the Company's merchandising program, and it was often featured in issues of *The
Red Barrel*.

The year 1924 saw the issue of a new tray. As with
previous designs, this tray had matching art on a calendar dated for the same year. Unique to this 1920s
tray issue are two slight variations of the tray,
although both show the same picture and both are
dated 1924. One tray has a dark brown rim and the
other has a lighter reddish-brown rim. Advanced serving
tray collectors seek out both varieties. Why different rim
colors were printed isn't known. Both of these
issues were printed, and are so marked, by
American Artworks, Coshocton, Ohio.

The tray dated and issued in 1925 featured a pretty lady wearing a white fox tail coat
and evening dress. Her fashion depicted the
best of the Roaring Twenties look. This issue
has been dubbed the "Party Girl" tray by collectors, undoubtedly due to the appearance in the background of a scene depicting a social gathering. A calendar with
matching artwork was also issued that same year. As with the 1923 and 1924 trays,
American Artworks printed this attractive serving tray. The artwork was also used in
magazine advertisements of the day.

Through the years, The Coca-Cola Company used many different models for
their artwork. Several individuals have claimed that they knew of a grandmother, or
an acquaintance, who had actually modeled for a given tray. One woman claimed,
for instance, that she had been the model for the 1914 "Betty" tray, and was quite

*1926 cardboard cutout, 18" by 32". Pretty girls
in swimsuits were popular images during the 1920s.
This example featuring the slogan "7 Million Drinks
A Day" can be found in two variations, with the
model holding either a glass or a bottle.*

strident in her claims to being the original "Betty." Not knowing the actual date of issue of the tray, she claimed that her modeling work was done in 1921. The Coca-Cola Company Historical Archives department has had many such claims presented to them, but no one, to date, has been able to substantiate the accuracy of such conjecture. If one looks at the ladies pictured on the 1920-1924 tray issues, it would appear that they are arguably the same person. While there were actual models for certain trays, some may have simply been an artist's conception of a pretty young woman. Of course, there were also the early Hilda Clark and Lillian Nordica images, and likenesses of some movie personalities were used on later trays, but most models were apparently chosen for presenting the wholesome appearance desired in Coca-Cola advertising imagery.

The Company decided to change the look of its trays in 1926. Beginning with the 1926 issue, and continuing on until 1950, the trays had either a gold or silver band around the edge, with a red inner rim around the picture. There was a slightly different variation of this theme on the 1936 tray, but all of the other trays had the bright red inner rim. For that reason, the trays issued in those years (1926-1950) have become known to collectors as the "Red Rim Series," and are frequently collected as a distinct set of trays.

The 1926 tray reflected the art of Fred Mizen, a contemporary illustrator. Diverting from the pretty girl look, this tray, which is dated 1926, depicts a golf course scene with a young man dressed in a white suit serving a Coca-Cola to a woman who is dressed in a white outfit. Not surprisingly, collectors have appropriately deemed this the "Golfing Couple" tray. American Artworks produced this tray issue as well. While a calendar was also issued by Coca-Cola in 1926, for the first time in many years, its picture did not correspond to the artwork on the tray.

1927 brought still a different art theme to the serving tray. Two issues dated 1927 featured a "Soda Jerk" serving Coca-Cola. At some point in time, the term "soda jerk" was attached to the individual who served soda at a soda fountain by pulling the fountain handle dozens of times a day to dispense soft drinks. One tray version from 1927 pictures a young man dressed in a white coat and hat carrying three glasses of Coca-Cola. This tray has become properly known and indelibly inked in the minds of collectors as the "Soda Jerk" tray. The second design depicts a similarly dressed individual serving Coca-Cola to a couple in an automobile. Obviously intended to reflect a drive-in scene, this tray is unusual in that the image is printed horizontally rather than vertically. Only a few Coca-Cola serving trays were printed with a horizontal picture on them. Collectors have dubbed this the "Curb Service" tray—aptly describing the scene depicted on the tray.

For some reason, Coca-Cola chose American Artworks to print and produce the 1927 "Soda Jerk" tray, and another company named Tindeco to produce the "Curb Service" tray. The quality of printing of the Tindeco "Curb Service" tray is not remotely up to the standard of quality which American Artworks had established. "Curb Service" trays often exhibit yellowing of the finish coating, and a dullness in the overall picture not associated with American Artworks trays. It is, therefore, very difficult to locate exceptional examples of the 1927 "Curb Service" tray.

The 1928 serving tray pictures a young woman holding a bottle of Coca-Cola and sipping from a straw. Since her hair features the twenties bobbed-hair style, collectors have given this issue the title of "Bobbed Hair Girl" tray. Although issued as a tray in 1928, a 1927 copyright designation is printed on the tray, which dates the artwork. With the previous two trays obviously having been issued for the fountain service market, this tray was issued for the bottler. After using Tindeco to produce the "Curb Service" tray, the Company went back to American Artworks for production of the "Bobbed Hair Girl" tray. As with all of the trays printed and produced by American Artworks after 1923, the printer's designation is located at the center of the bottom edge of the picture. A Spanish language version of this tray was also issued, representing the first foreign-designated serving tray.

Recognizing two different markets for their products, Coca-Cola issued different trays for the fountain and bottler markets in the late 1920s. Not coincidentally, Coca-Cola bottle sales in 1928 surpassed fountain syrup sales for the first time in the Company's history.

In 1929, the Company issued two trays, each depicting the same girl wearing a swimsuit. Both are dated 1929. In the tray targeted for fountain sales, the young woman has a glass of Coca-Cola in her right hand. Printed by American Artworks, this tray reflects the high quality standards of this advertising production company. Contrastingly, the bottler version, which shows the same young lady holding a bottle instead of a glass, was printed by Tindeco, and it is marked as such. High-quality specimens of this tray are extremely rare. Most exhibit a picture in which the image lacks sharpness and, for some reason, the gold ink on the rim appears to have oxidized over a period of years, turning the rim from gold to a drab, dark brown color. Fortunately, The Coca-Cola Company never again selected Tindeco to produce its advertising serving trays.

The twenties provided a treasure trove of serving trays for collectors. As with the earliest serving trays, their art mirrored the life style and fashions of the time. Given the impetus of a vibrant economy and brilliant merchandising during this period, The Coca-Cola Company continued its dynamic growth in sales. By 1928, there

1928 cardboard sign, 21 1/2" by 32".
1928 was the first year sales of Coca-Cola in bottles surpassed sales of fountain syrup.

were 1,263 franchised bottlers and 108,000 soda fountains selling Coca-Cola. The Company had expanded its boundaries to the point that there were 64 bottlers operating in 28 countries outside the United States, and a marketing arm was established just for promotion of foreign sales. Advertising expenditures totaled $3,900,000 in 1929.

From an overall merchandising standpoint, the Company continued to add many new and innovative ways to promote its product in the 1920s. With the emergence of the automobile as the primary mode of transportation in the United States, outdoor advertising by Coca-Cola was greatly expanded. In 1925, the first full-color billboard was used, and soon they appeared throughout the country. In big cities, large illuminated signs also were first used in 1929. Whether in a rural setting or a large metropolitan area, Coca-Cola was promoted everywhere with compelling and colorful images.

In addition to its continued and growing preeminence in merchandising and promotion during the 1920s, the Company introduced important new packaging concepts such as the handy six-pack carton, which helped create huge new market opportunities. Just over the horizon were still more innovations destined to add an even greater dimension to the dynamic growth of Coca-Cola.

1920 SERVING TRAY
(RECTANGULAR)
PTR 027.000

Although ushering in a new decade, the 1920 tray proved to be a throwback to previous years when a variety of sizes and types of a single artwork design were used. This issue, which is referred to as the "Golfer Girl" tray due to artwork picturing a golf setting with a girl holding a glass of Coca-Cola, was produced in a rectangular design, a change tray (the last one issued), and a large oval sized tray. Unlike most tray issues, the 1920 trays did not have the name of a printer indicated on them. The rectangular tray pictured here was issued in a 10 1/2-inch by 13 1/4-inch size. From this point on all future trays would be issued in the rectangular size of 10 1/2 inches by 13 1/4 inches. In addition to the three tray issues, this identical artwork was used on the 1920 calendar, and a pocket mirror. All of the trays are marked "Copyright Coca-Cola Company" on their face.

1920 SERVING TRAY
(OVAL)
PT0 027.000

With artwork identical to that of the rectangular 1920 tray and calendar, an oval-sized tray measuring 13 3/4 inches by 16 3/4 inches was also issued. This issue, which is referred to as the "Golfer Girl" tray due to artwork picturing a golf setting with a girl holding a glass of Coca-Cola, was produced in a rectangular design, a change tray (the last one issued), and the large, oval-sized tray pictured here. As with the other 1920 tray issues, the name of the printer does not appear on the tray. In addition to the three tray issues, this identical artwork was used on the 1920 calendar and a pocket mirror.

1920 CHANGE TRAY
PTT 027.000

Issued in a 4 1/2-inch by 6 3/8-inch oval size, this change tray was produced with the same artwork as the 1920 large oval serving tray. It proved to be the last change tray ever issued by The Coca-Cola Company. As with the other trays issued in 1920, there is no printer's identification noted, but it does bear the inscription "Copyright Coca-Cola Company" on the bottom edge of the picture. In addition to the three tray issues, this identical artwork was used on the 1920 calendar and a pocket mirror.

1921 SERVING TRAY
PTR 028.000

This tray is nicknamed the "Autumn Girl" or "Navy Girl" tray due to artwork depicting a young lady holding a glass of Coca-Cola, while seated in front of a tree. She is wearing a hat reminiscent of a Navy hat. No printer is designated on the tray, but it is dated 1921 due to the use of identical artwork on the 1921 calendar. The tray is marked "Copyright Coca-Cola Company" on the edge of the picture, and was issued in a 10 1/2-inch x 13 1/4-inch rectangular size.

1922 SERVING TRAY
PTR 029.000

The 1922 tray issue is referred to by collectors as the "Summer Girl" tray. Dated 1921, and marked as being printed by "H.D. Beech Co., Coshocton O." on the lower edge of the picture, this tray was actually made for distribution in 1922, along with a calendar for that same year with matching artwork. The calendar is a favorite of collectors because it shows not only the girl pictured on the tray, but a baseball game scene as well. The tray design is unique among Coca-Cola tray art in that it has little square gold dots on the rim surrounding the picture. Issued in a 10 1/2-inch by 13 1/4-inch rectangular size, the artwork was only known to have been used on one other advertising piecc, that being the 1922 calendar.

1923 SERVING TRAY
PTR 030.000

This tray, which has become known as the "Flapper Girl" tray, depicts a young lady dressed party-style in typical upscale 1920s fashion. Issued in a 10 1/2-inch by 13 1/4-inch rectangular size, identification markings on the original tray include "©coca-cola co. 1923, american artworks, inc. coshocton, o." and "made in u. s. a." on the bottom edge of the picture. In the early 1970s, The Coca-Cola Company issued a series of reproduction trays which included the 1923 design. To differentiate the reproduction trays from the originals, the trademark notation, which was present in the tail of the large "C" of the word Coca-Cola on the original tray, was not shown on the reproduction. Also, the reproduction tray did not include the designation of the printer of the original trays (American Artworks, inc.). Artwork used on the 1923 tray was also used on the 1923 calendar.

1924 SERVING TRAY
PTR 031.001

This tray is difficult to locate relative to its date of issue and is referred to as the "Smiling Girl" tray. It was issued in two versions with identical artwork. One version had a brown rim (depicted here) and the other had a reddish or burgundy red rim. Of the two, the reddish version is the least common. Issued in a 10 1/2-inch by 13 1/4-inch rectangular size, identification markings on the trays include "©coca-cola co. 1924, american artworks, inc. coshocton, o." and "made in u. s. a." on the bottom edge of the picture. Artwork depicted on this tray was also used on the 1924 calendar. Additional usage of this artwork included a needle holder, a print media ad, and a cardboard cutout.

1924 SERVING TRAY
PTR 030.002

This tray is difficult to locate relative to its date of issue, and is referred to as the "Smiling Girl" tray. It was issued in two versions which showed identical artwork. One version had a brown rim, and the other, a reddish or burgundy red rim. Of the two, the reddish version is the most uncommon. Issued in a 10 1/2 inches by 13 1/4 inches rectangular size, identification markings on the trays include "coca-cola co. 1924, american artworks, inc. coshocton, o." and "made in u.s.a." on the bottom edge of the picture. Artwork depicted on this tray was also used on the 1924 calendar. Additional usage of this artwork included a needle holder, a print media ad, and a cardboard cutout. *This is the red rim version.*

1925 SERVING TRAY
PTR 032.000

This tray has become known as the "Party Girl" tray due to its artwork depicting a young woman in a formal twenties-style dress at a party scene. Issued in a 10 1/2-inch by 13 1/4-inch rectangular size, identification markings on the original tray include "©coca-cola co. 1925, american artworks, inc. coshocton, o." and "made in u. s. a." on the bottom edge of the picture. In the early 1970s The Coca-Cola Company issued a series of reproduction trays which included the 1925 design. To differentiate the reproduction trays from the originals, the trademark notation which was present in the tail of the large "C" of the word Coca-Cola on the original tray was not included on the reproduction. The reproduction tray also did not include the designation of the printer of the original trays (American Artworks, inc.). This same artwork was also used on the 1925 calendar, a needle holder, and a print media ad.

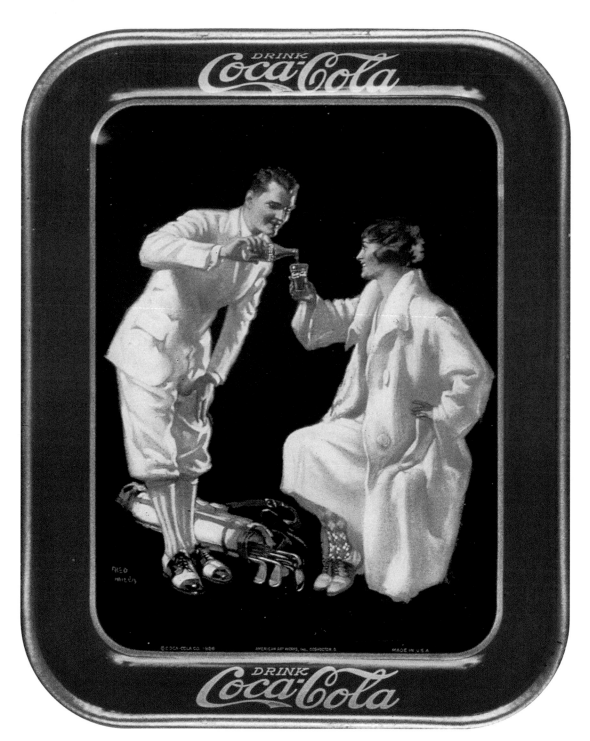

1926 SERVING TRAY
PTR 033.000

This tray, which depicts a young couple sharing a Coca-Cola while engaged in a round of golf, features the artwork of illustrator Fred Mizen. Commonly known as the "Golfing Couple" tray, it was issued in a 10 1/2-inch by 13 1/4-inch rectangular size. Identification markings on the original tray include "©coca-cola co.1926, american art works, inc. coshocton, o." and "made in u. s. a." on the bottom edge of the picture. In addition to being a popular tray with collectors, this issue also was the first of what has become known as the "red rim" tray series, due to the use of a red inner rim and gold, or silver, outer rim. This was common to all trays issued from 1926-1942, with the exception of the 1936 tray. The 1926 tray's outer rim is gold. A reproduction has been made of this tray in a different format, and in a larger rectangular size—readily identifiable from the original. This same art was featured in print media advertising during in the late 1920s.

1927 SERVING TRAY
PTR 034.000

This issue is known to collectors as the "Curb Service" tray due to its artwork featuring a drive-up fountain service attendant serving Coca-Cola to a couple in a car. It measures 13 1/4 inches by 10 1/2 inches, and is formatted in a horizontal design. Unlike all but one other of the trays produced in the red-rim series (1926-1942), it was printed by a company other than American Art Works, and is marked "©1927 by coca-cola co., tindeco," and "made in u. s. a." on the lower edge of the picture. Tindeco also produced the 1929 bottle version tray. The trays produced by Tindeco were substandard and inconsistent, making it difficult to find an example of this tray that is comparable in quality to those produced by American Art Works.

1927 SERVING TRAY
PTR 035.000

Also produced and distributed the same year as the "Curb Service" tray, this issue is referred to by collectors as the "Soda Jerk" tray. The term "soda jerk" referred to an individual who served sodas and other related items at fountain services, which were very popular at the time. As with earlier rectangular issues, the tray measures 10 1/2 inches by 13 1/4 inches. The markings on the lower edge of the picture are: "©coca-cola co.1927, american art works, inc. coshocton, o." and "made in u. s. a." This same artwork was also featured in print media ads.

1928 SERVING TRAY
PTR 036.000

This tray features the image of a girl sipping Coca-Cola from a bottle. Over the years, it has become known as the "Bobbed Hair Girl" tray due to the young woman's hair style which was popular in the 1920s. Although the tray was issued in 1928, it is actually dated 1927. Typical of other rectangular issues, the tray measures 10 1/2 inches by 13 1/4 inches. The markings on the lower edge of lower edge of the picture are: "©coca-cola co. 1927, american art works, inc. coshocton, o." and "made in u. s. a." This tray was also issued in a Spanish language version, and, as such, is the first-known tray to have been produced for foreign markets. The artwork on this tray was also featured on a deck of cards.

1929 SERVING TRAY
BOTTLE VERSION
PTR 037.002

Two trays were issued this same year, with nearly identical artwork depicting a girl in a swimsuit sitting down enjoying a Coca-Cola. The one pictured here is known as the "bottle version" and was produced by Tindeco—the same company that produced the 1927 "Curb Service" tray. Produced specifically for the bottler market, this tray depicts a girl holding a bottle of Coca-Cola. This rectangular tray measures 10 1/2 inches by 13 1/4 inches. The tray is marked "©1929 by coca-cola co., tindeco," and "made in u. s. a." on the lower edge of the picture. Due to the inferiority of the printing process used by Tindeco, it is difficult to find an attractive and desirable example of this particular tray.

1929 SERVING TRAY
GLASS VERSION
PTR 037.001

This tray depicts virtually the same art as the 1929 "bottle version" tray, except that it shows the girl holding a glass rather than a bottle. Produced for the fountain service market, this rectangular tray measures 10 1/2 inches by 13 1/4 inches, and is characterized by the same high-quality printing definition and colors customary to trays produced by American Artworks. The markings on the lower edge of the picture are: "©coca-cola co.1929, american art works, inc. coshocton, o." and "made in u. s. a."

CHAPTER SIX

TRAY ISSUES OF THE 1930s

I n the final years of the 1920s, Coca-Cola engineered and designed its first officially issued Coca-Cola cooler, now referred to as the "Glascock Cooler." While not refrigerated, the cooler had doors on the top which allowed the vendor to place ice inside to chill the Coca-Cola bottles. The metal cooler was adorned in attractive red and green colors, which advertised the drink and afforded gas stations and stores the perfect way to offer patrons a cold Coca-Cola. Available for only $12.50 from bottlers, this cooler was an ideal innovation for an increasingly mobile society where automotive travel was becoming a way of life.

While genius in packaging was leading the way to greater growth of the Company, the serving tray continued to be an important part of Coca-Cola merchandising. The thirties would see tray issues for each year of the decade. To lead things off, the Company ushered in 1930 with two tray designs. One targeted the soda fountain market, with artwork depicting a young woman talking on the telephone. Advertising copy on the red rim tray implores "Meet me at the soda fountain." This tray has become known to collectors as the "Telephone Girl" tray.

The tray developed for bottler distribution depicts a pretty young lady, dressed in a white swimsuit and red cap, holding a bottle of Coca-Cola. It is noteworthy that while most of the bather trays have the bright red rim consistent with the red rim series, these authors have seen a couple of nearly perfect swimsuit trays sporting a deep orange-colored rim. Whether this was done intentionally, or was simply the result of an improper paint formula, is unknown. The artwork for the "bather tray," as it has been nicknamed, was done by the noted illustrator, Haddon Sundblom. Sundblom ranks as the most prolific artist in the history of Coca-Cola advertising, as his work was used by the Company for more than forty years.

The year 1930 was the last in which The Coca-Cola Company issued two tray designs for the same year. Every tray issued from that point on showed a bottle

Left: 1930 cardboard cutout, 18" by 42". This beautiful image of a girl in a white swimsuit was done by Haddon Sundblom, and was also used on a serving tray for 1930.

rather than a glass—clearly demonstrating the growing market for bottled Coca-Cola. Both of the trays issued in 1930 are dated and marked as having been produced by American Artworks, of Coshocton, Ohio.

The year 1931 saw the issue of a tray which has proven to be among the most popular with collectors. Coca-Cola commissioned Norman Rockwell, one of America's most famous illustrators, to paint a series of six art works which would be used to promote its products. The first of these was used for the 1931 calendar and serving tray. Rockwell's artwork was based on Whittier's famous poem "The Barefoot Boy," and it depicts a young farm boy in a straw hat sitting beside his dog. The boy holds a bottle of Coca-Cola in one hand and a sandwich in the other. Collectors have most frequently referred to this tray as the "Rockwell Tray."

The model for this tray was Dan Mac Grant, who still resides in Los Angeles. *The Red Barrel* issue of April 1931 contains an interesting article on the subject of this tray and the matching calendar artwork created by Rockwell. It states the following:

"A tenderfoot scout who is in the seventh grade at the Los Angeles Public School, and who catches for his school baseball team when he is not working in the movies, is the 'Barefoot Boy' of the most popular Coca-Cola calendar ever issued.

"Danny Mac Grant, whose broad smile is framed in the setting of many freckles and honest to goodness red hair, posed for the Norman Rockwell painting reproduced on the calendar.

"To date, more than 1,800,000, (calendars) have been distributed suggesting many times every day the pause that refreshes in as many homes, offices, stores, schools and other gathering places.

"The same illustration also appeared on the April 24 sheet poster, on the Coca-Cola tray and was used for the Bottler's window display.

"His broad, boyish smile and wealth of freckles and red hair, won him the job of posing for Mr. Rockwell, when the artist was brought face to face with four boys picked from studio photographs. The posing was done in April, 1930, and required five days."

—*The Red Barrel,* April, 1931

No records exist regarding the number of 1931 trays actually produced, but it is likely that the quantity was similar to that of the calendar distribution of nearly two million. Although in great demand, this tray is far more available today than the next two issues produced after the start of the Great Depression.

The 1932 tray continued a well-established art choice for Coca-Cola serving trays—a pretty young woman in a swimsuit. From 1929 until 1939, seven tray issues

1936 tin embossed sign, 16". In 1936, The Coca-Cola Company celebrated its 50th anniversary. This tin sign was one of the many pieces used to commemorate the occasion. Anything associated with the 50th anniversary is very popular with collectors.

featured young ladies in swimsuits. This one is a particular favorite of the author. Several nicknames have been attached to this tray by collectors over the years, including the "Swimsuit Girl" tray, and "Girl in the Yellow Bathing Suit" tray. The model bears an amazing resemblance to Marilyn Monroe (who, of course, wasn't of modeling age at that time), but regardless, the likeness is striking. Hayden-Hayden, another well-known illustrator of the time, created the artwork for this tray. It was offered to bottlers for 13 1/4¢ each, in boxes of 50.

Collectors searching for this tray and the one issued in 1933 will find that high-quality examples are difficult to locate. This is, undoubtedly, a result of the Depression, when bottlers, like other businesses, were struggling just to stay afloat, and when discretionary funds for advertising were limited.

The late 1920s and 1930s brought about a distinct effort on the part of the Company to seek out and use advertising illustrations that might be truly regarded

1932 cardboard cutout, 10" by 16", featuring movie star Dorothy Mackaill. The early to mid-1930s were boom years for Hollywood, and The Coca-Cola Company showcased many of the stars of the silver screen.

as works of art. Fred Mizen, Bradshaw Crandell, Norman Rockwell, Haddon Sundblom, Hayden-Hayden, McClelland Barclay, N. C. Wyeth, and Fredrick Stanley were all prominent illustrators who created wonderful artwork for Coca-Cola. Today, original paintings done for The Coca-Cola Company by these artists bring astounding prices in the original American Art marketplace.

Yet another Coca-Cola Company innovation was unveiled at the Chicago World's Fair, in 1933. Visitors to the fair were treated to Coca-Cola dispensed from a machine that automatically mixed carbonated water and the syrup. From that point on, manual mixing of the syrup and soda water became a thing of the past. During the same period, refrigerated stand-alone coolers for bottles of Coca-Cola were being improved and perfected. By 1935, the first refrigerated cooler vending machine was offered to retailers. Automation would fuel the engine for further Coca-Cola Company growth in the thirties and beyond.

The 1933 tray was the first since the 1905 Lillian Nordica edition to feature a celebrity. Frances Dee, a motion picture actress, is pictured in a swimsuit. This tray is dated 1933, and states "Frances Dee—Paramount Player" in the left-hand corner. The Company had obviously experienced a poor level of bottler and fountain service orders for the 1932 tray, so the price of the 1933 tray was adjusted to its lowest in many years—12 1/2¢ each—to stimulate demand when the national economy was at its low point.

Celebrities took center stage in Coca-Cola advertising art in the 1930s. Jean Harlow, Cary Grant, Frances Dee, Madge Evans, Sue Carol, Maureen O'Sullivan, and others were pictured in advertisements promoting Coca-Cola. The Company even had its own traveling band. Radio ads featuring celebrities were common.

With celebrities becoming a centerpiece of Coca-Cola advertising art, the 1934 tray featured horizontal artwork with movie luminaries. Johnny Weissmuller and Maureen O'Sullivan are pictured in swimsuits, toasting each other with a bottle of Coca-Cola. Since Weissmuller was featured as Tarzan in the movies, collectors over the years have referred to this tray as the "Tarzan" tray. Although less scarce than the trays of the two previous years, this tray has always commanded a premium in the collector marketplace due to the subject matter and tie-in to the movies. The artwork for this tray was produced from a photo maintained in The Coca-Cola Company archives.

In 1935, Madge Evans, a Metro-Goldwyn-Mayer player in the movies, was featured on the tray edition for that year. Shown in a festive party scene wearing a stunning white dress and holding a glass of Coca-Cola, the tray is very colorful. As with all of the thirties trays, it is dated for the year of issue.

In 1936, Coca-Cola issued a tray which has become known as the "Hostess Girl" tray. The artwork, created by Hayden-Hayden, also was used on a large cardboard sign. One of the more stunning of the thirties trays, the woman pictured is adorned in a white evening dress. She is reclining, and holding a glass of Coca-Cola. Unlike the other trays in the red rim series, this tray has a red outer edge rim with a gold inner rim. The colors are striking, and add to the individuality of the tray's look. A French language version of the tray was also produced.

Another swimsuit girl was featured on the 1937 tray. Shown running along a beach and holding a bottle of Coca-Cola in each hand, the young lady is depicted in a yellow bathing suit, with a thin translucent cape attached to her neck. A cardboard advertising sign with this same artwork also exists. One of this book's authors had the opportunity to meet a woman who had viable claims to being the model for this tray. Without specific documentation or a contract to substantiate her assertion, she recalled having posed in the late 1930s for Rolf Armstrong (a prominent illustrator). Armstrong had stated that the painting for which she posed was meant for use by The Coca-Cola Company. Josephine Moore, the individual who made the claim, recalled being dressed in a swimsuit and standing in place on the tip of her right foot, in a pose intended to simulate running. Several years later, she saw the 1937 serving tray and was sure the picture she had posed for was the art for that piece.

Further adding to Josephine Moore's credentials were scrapbook pictures and magazine articles displaying photos of her modeling for Rubbermaid swimsuits, Chevrolet automobiles, a beer company, and several other firms. Even more compelling to the veracity of her claim is the striking similarity between pictures of her taken in the late thirties, and the face of the young woman depicted on the 1937 serving tray. Using the motion picture stage name, Verna Clair, for MGM, and hav-

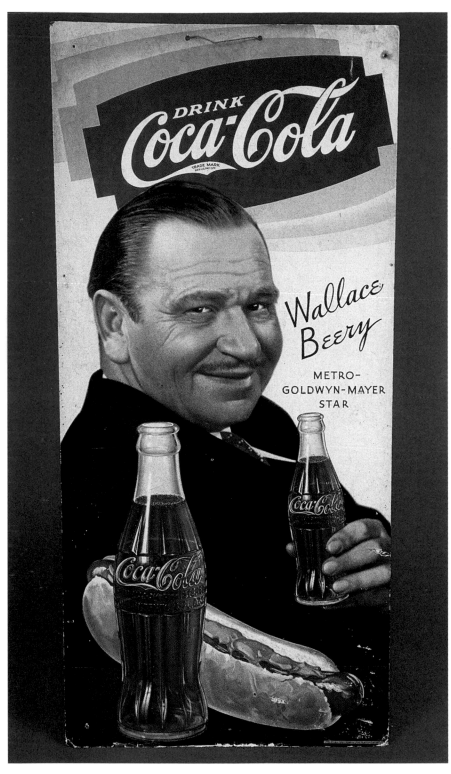

1934 cardboard sign, 14" by 30", featuring one of the biggest stars of the 1930s, Wallace Beery. Beery also appeared on a cardboard cutout window display along with Jackie Cooper. The pair were stars of M.G.M.'s 1934 classic, Treasure Island.

ing succeeded as a prominent model in the appropriate time period, it is unlikely that Mrs. Moore would have had a motive to fabricate her story. Mrs. Moore was in her mid-seventies and still quite beautiful in 1990 when the author met with her. At that time, she resided near Placerville, California, with her husband, a prominent retired judge.

The 1938 serving tray featured the artwork of illustrator Bradshaw Crandell. Known by collectors today as the "Girl at Shade," the tray depicts an attractive woman sitting in front of a window shade. She is adorned in a stylish hat and dress, and is holding a bottle of Coca-Cola. Issued in large quantities, this tray remains readily available to collectors today. Additional versions were produced in French-Canadian and English-Canadian.

Closing out the tray issues of the 1930s was the 1939 tray, which pictures a pretty young woman sitting on a diving board. She is wearing a white swimsuit, and holding up a bottle of Coca-Cola. With colorful artwork typical of the trays of that period, the artist for this tray was the well-known Haddon Sundblom. The same design was also produced in a Spanish version.

As with the twenties, the decade of the thirties saw The Coca-Cola Company reach for, and attain, new heights. Advertising was upscale, with celebrities in vogue. New communication tools, such as radio, were widely used to promote Coca-Cola. Slogans such as "the pause that refreshes" were seen everywhere. In 1939, a record fifty million gallons of Coca-Cola were sold. Annual advertising expenditures exceeded $7,000,000, and in the five-year period from 1934 to 1939, a total of 74,500 Coca-Cola refrigerated coolers were sold. The automatic fountain dispenser added a whole new dimension to sales opportunities as well. The Company had not only weathered the Great Depression, but had actually thrived during it. Still another decade passed in which the advertising serving tray remained an established staple in The Company's promotional arsenal.

1930 SERVING TRAY
PTR 038.000

As in 1929, two trays were issued in 1930. The one shown here was for the fountain service market, which is noted by use of the prominent slogan "Meet me at the soda fountain." Commonly referred to as the "Telephone Girl" tray by collectors, it measures 10 1/2 inches by 13 1/4 inches, and bears markings on the lower edge of the picture as follows: "©coca-cola co. 1930 american art works, inc. coshocton, o." and "made in u. s. a."

1930 SERVING TRAY
PTR 039.000

The second tray issued in 1930 was designated for distribution by bottlers. It featured a swimsuit girl holding a bottle of Coca-Cola, and was produced in a rectangular size measuring 10 1/2 inches by 13 1/4 inches. The markings on the lower edge of the picture are: "©coca-cola co.1930, american art works, inc. coshocton, o." and "made in u. s. a." The same artwork was also featured on a cardboard cutout.

1931 SERVING TRAY
PTR 040.000

The 1931 tray features the art of Norman Rockwell and, as such, is a favorite among collectors. Based on original art entitled "The Barefoot Boy," the tray is also referred to by collectors as the "Rockwell Tray." It was produced in a rectangular size measuring 10 1/2 inches by 13 1/4 inches. The markings on the lower edge of the picture are: "©coca-cola co.1931, american art works, inc. coshocton, o." and "made in u. s. a." The company also produced calendars and other items with this same artwork.

1932 SERVING TRAY
PTR 041.000

Continuing a tradition which started with the 1929 tray design, the 1932 tray was another of the six issues which featured swimsuit girls. This specific one is sometimes referred to as the "Girl in Yellow Bathing Suit" tray. It features a swimsuit girl holding a bottle of Coca-Cola, and was produced in a rectangular size measuring 10 1/2 inches by 13 1/4 inches. The markings on the lower edge of the picture are: "©coca-cola co.1932, american art works, inc. coshocton o." and "made in u.s.a." The tray also reflects the artist's signature (Hayden-Hayden) in the lower left hand corner of the picture.

1933 SERVING TRAY
PTR 042.000

For the first time since 1905, a Coca-Cola tray featured a celebrity. The 1933 tray is referred to as the "Frances Dee" tray because it depicts the star in a swimsuit, with identification on the lower left edge of the picture stating, "Frances Dee Paramount Player." The tray was produced in a rectangular size measuring 10 1/2 inches by 13 1/4 inches. The markings on the lower edge of the picture are: "©coca-cola co.1933, american art works, inc. coshocton o." and "made in u.s.a."

1934 SERVING TRAY
PTR 043.000

This tray has dual collector appeal due to its depiction of the actors who played in a very popular *Tarzan* movie. In addition to the normal markings, the tray presents the statement "Maureen O'Sullivan and Johnny Weissmuller (Metro-Goldwin Mayer Featured Players)" on the lower right hand side of the picture. Over the years, this has become known as the "Weissmuller" tray. It measures 13 1/4 inches by 10 1/2 inches, and is formatted in a horizontal design. The markings on the lower edge of the picture are: "©coca-cola co.1934, american art works, inc. coshocton o." and "made in u.s.a." A reproduction of this tray has often been misrepresented as an original. The reproduction does not include the American Artworks notation, and the image and colors (particularly the rim which is not bright gold like the original) are much less distinct when the two are held side by side.

1935 SERVING TRAY
PTR 044.000

Referenced by collectors as the "Madge Evans" tray, this issue was another in a brief series of trays featuring celebrities. The tray was produced in a rectangular size measuring 10 1/2 inches by 13 1/4 inches. The markings on the lower edge of the picture are:

"©coca-cola co.1935, american art works, inc. coshocton o." and "made in u.s.a." On the lower part of Madge Evans' dress is the notation "Madge Evans-Metro Goldwin Mayer Player."

1936 SERVING TRAY
PTR 045.000

Known as the "Hostess" tray by collectors, the image for this attractive issue was created by artist Hayden-Hayden. Unlike all of the other red-rim series trays (1926-1942), the rim colors on this issue were inverted, featuring a gold inner-rim and a red outer-edge rim. The tray was produced in a rectangular size measuring 10 1/2 inches by 13 1/4 inches. The markings on the lower edge of the picture are: "©coca-cola co. 1936, american art works, inc. co-shocton o." and "made in u.s.a." A French language version and a Canadian-English variation of this tray were also produced. Additionally, the same artwork appeared on a cardboard sign issued in the same year.

1937 SERVING TRAY
PTR 046.000

This issue is referred to by collectors as the "Running Girl" tray due to the artwork showing a girl running on the beach. It measures 10 1/2 inches by 13 1/4 inches, and bears markings on the lower edge of the picture as follows: "©coca-cola co. 1937 american art works, inc. coshocton, o." and "made in u. s. a." A reproduction of this tray was produced in the 1970s, but it does not provide the name of the printer, nor the crisp and sharp images of the original. The Company also produced a cardboard sign with the same artwork for issue in 1937 as well.

1938 SERVING TRAY
PTR 047.000

Known by collectors today as the "Girl at Shade" tray, this issue featured the artwork of illustrator Bradshaw Crandell, whose signature is noted on the lower right edge of the picture. The tray was produced in a rectangular size measuring 10 1/2 inches by 13 1/4 inches. The markings on the lower edge of the picture are: "©coca-cola co.1938, american art works, inc. coshocton o." and "made in u.s.a." Additional versions were produced for the Canadian market in English and French.

1939 SERVING TRAY
PTR 048.000

With artwork created by the well-known illustrator Haddon Sundblom, this was the last year in which a tray featured a swim-suit girl. Known by collectors as the "Springboard Girl" tray, it measures 10 1/2 inches by 13 1/4 inches and bears markings on the lower edge of the picture as follows: "©coca-cola co. 1939 american art works, inc. coshocton, o." and "made in u. s. a." The outer rim is silver, and the inner red rim contains thin silver lines (earlier red-rim tray issues featured gold rims). The artist's signature (Sundblom) appears on the lower edge of the picture. A Spanish version of this tray was also produced—as well as a large cardboard sign with matching artwork in 1939.

Created in 1942, the image of "The Sprite" is now known as "The Sprite Boy" by collectors. Used extensively during the 1940s and 1950s, he can be found wearing a bottle cap when promoting bottle sales, and a soda jerk cap when promoting fountain sales.

CHAPTER SEVEN

TRAY ISSUES OF THE 1940s

The 1940s presented new challenges to The Coca-Cola Company. Hostilities erupted in Europe, and quickly evolved into World War II after Japan's 1941 attack on Pearl Harbor. Due to the war effort, sugar, a key ingredient in the Coca-Cola formula, was placed on restriction and rationed at fifty percent of the pre-war average. Because of the sugar shortage in the U. S., the Company boldly expanded its foreign operations to the point that 64 additional bottling plants were installed to make the drink available to troops stationed in various foreign markets. Without the ability to further expand production in the United States due to the sugar restriction, the Company rapidly moved to develop its global strategy.

Coca-Cola advertisements displayed patriotic themes highlighted by pictures of servicemen drinking Coca-Cola. Cardboard signs, calendars, and magazine advertisements exhibited soldiers at work and returning home on leave to their wives or girlfriends. By this time, Coca-Cola was as American as hamburgers and apple pie, and advertising for the product continually emphasized that symbolic trilogy. One ad featured the slogan "Coca-Cola–the global high-sign," stressing the point that the man in uniform would be greeted everywhere with the drink that stood for happy comradeship. To further build its business, the Company sponsored music programs on radio, which were broadcast to more than 43 military bases across the United States.

The serving tray, which had played a prominent part in Coca-Cola advertising in the years from 1897 to 1940, was dealt a severe blow by the war effort. The metal shortage, which had impacted tray issues in World War I as well, reoccurred, and had an even more pronounced effect in the forties. Manufacturers in all sectors were asked to avoid production requiring metal that could more appropriately be used for munitions. Consequently, Coca-Cola produced prodigious numbers of colorful cardboard signs which have become highly sought after by today's collectors of Coca-Cola advertising memorabilia. Only three tray designs were issued in the 1940s, and all of them were produced in the first three years of the decade.

The tray issued in 1940 featured art which collectors have appropriately named the "Sailor Girl." The picture is composed in a horizontal layout, and depicts a young lady holding a bottle of Coca-Cola. She is shown sitting with a fishing pole on a boat dock, and wearing a white sailor hat. The outer edge of the rim is silver, in contrast to most of the 1930s trays which had a gold-edged rim. A few of these trays have shown up with a gold rim, but the vast majority have the silver rim. The inner red rim also reflects the use of thin silver lines contrasted to the red. This minor variation is a first for tray issues. The art for this tray was also used on a cardboard poster, in magazine ads, and on other Coca-Cola advertising materials. The tray was also produced in French-Canadian and English-Canadian versions.

Emphasizing the theme that Coca-Cola was a year-round drink, the 1941 serving tray design featured a young lady ice skater, seated on a log and holding a bottle of Coca-Cola, while taking a breather during an outing. Known today as the "Skater Girl" tray, the artwork also featured the "silhouette girl" logo in the red border. This tray displays a gold outer-edge rim, and like other trays, it is very colorful. A large cardboard poster displays the same artwork, and there was additional use of this picture on other advertising items.

The 1942 serving tray is a favorite of collectors. Referred to as the "Two Girls at Car" tray, the art features a young woman sitting in a convertible automobile, talking to another pretty lady who is standing next to the car, while both are enjoying a bottle of Coca-Cola. This tray has become popular with antique car buffs as well as collectors of Coca-Cola advertising. With a silver-edged rim, the tray has the same thin silver lines inside the red rim portion as were used on the 1940 tray. In addition to being the last tray issued by Coca-Cola in the 1940s, the 1942 tray was also the last tray to be produced by American Artworks, of Coshocton, Ohio.

American Artworks, which had been a major supplier of metal signs and serving trays to The Coca-Cola Company from 1910-1942, went out of business in 1950. Undoubtedly, the demise of the firm was related to the metal shortage in the early forties, which must have drastically reduced its potential market for printed metal advertising items.

Other influences contributed to the decline of the serving tray as a promotion tool for Coca-Cola beyond the thirties. While soda fountains were still in evidence and prospering, bottle sales by the Company were dramatically exceeding fountain sales. Very little advertising was produced that focused on the soda fountain. Consequently, the serving tray was starting to outlive its functional purpose. Although the war ended in 1945, the lingering effects of the metal shortage continued. Coca-Cola chose not to issue new serving trays in the remaining years of the forties. Radio and print media advertising, large billboards, and cardboard posters were adequately carrying the message for Coca-Cola. In spite of the war, the Company continued to prosper, and had, by necessity, continually expanded its international sales operations.

The post-war home building boom, combined with an economy which had put the depression behind it, created new marketing opportunities for Coca-Cola. The new slogan "It's the Real Thing" was born, joining earlier slogans in adding to the success of the drink. Another new tool for the company was television. Motion picture imagery could now be used to promote Coca-Cola to people in their own homes. With television, the possibilities for marketing innovations were virtually endless and, of course, The Coca-Cola Company demonstrated its creative genius in this area as well.

1940 SERVING TRAY
PTR 049.000

Collectors have named this the "Sailor Girl" tray due to its image of a young girl wearing a sailor's cap while sitting on a dock and holding a fishing pole. It measures 13 1/4 inches by 10 1/2 inches, and is formatted in a horizontal design. The markings on the lower edge of the picture are: "©coca-cola co.1940, american art works, inc. coshocton o." and "made in u.s.a." The outer rim is silver, and the inner red rim contains thin silver lines identical to those on the 1939 tray. The tray was also produced in French- and English-Canadian versions. The same artwork was used for a variety of other advertising materials.

1941 SERVING TRAY
PTR 050.000

To emphasize that Coca-Cola is not just a summer drink, the 1941 tray was produced with art depicting a girl in a winter skating scene. Collectors have come to refer to this as the "Skater Girl" tray. Typical of most of the red-rim series trays, this issue featured a gold outer rim and a solid red inner rim. There is one variation unique to this tray. The inclusion of the widely used "silhouette girl" symbol within the red rim on both sides of the picture. The tray was produced in a rectangular size measuring 10 1/2 inches by 13 1/4 inches. The markings on the lower edge of the picture are: "©coca-cola co.1941, american art works, inc. coshocton o." and "made in u.s.a." A large cardboard poster was just one of several advertising items that utilized the same artwork.

1942 SERVING TRAY
PTR 051.000

Known as the "Two Girls at Car" tray, this tray art features two girls enjoying Coca-Cola in a setting that includes a convertible car. Like the 1939 and 1940 trays, the outer rim is silver and the inner red rim contains thin silver lines. It measures 10 1/2 inches by 13 1/4 inches, and bears markings on the lower edge of the picture as follows: "©coca-cola co. 1942 american art works, inc. coshocton, o." and "made in u. s. a." This tray was the last one produced by American Artworks. It was also the last tray issued by The Coca-Cola Company in the 1940s.

COPYRIGHT 1951, THE COCA-COLA COMPANY   LITHO IN U.S.A.   SNYDER & BLACK, N.Y.   FORM NO. 1-91

Pretty girls enjoying sports and leisure activities were popular subject matter during the 1950s and 1960s.

CHAPTER EIGHT

TRAY ISSUES OF THE 1950s & 1960s

The fifties saw the addition of a few more serving tray issues. The first appeared in 1950. Referred to, today, as the "Girl with Wind in Hair" tray, the artwork depicts a young redheaded lady holding a bottle of Coca-Cola. The reference to "Girl with Wind in Hair" undoubtedly results from the appearance of the model's hair blowing in the wind. There is no designation of the firm that produced the tray. Two design versions of the tray exist. The first, and most common, has a green background for the picture which is lighter near the bottom half of the tray and darker near the top. The second depicts the same girl, but has a uniform, solid, dark-green background. The first version is significantly more common and must have been produced in a much greater quantity.

The 1950 tray was sold to bottlers for the sum of twenty four cents, and the artwork was created by Haddon Sundblom, an artist who had done many pieces of art work for The Company. The tray was also produced in Canadian issues, which included French- and English-Canadian versions.

The second fifties tray was first produced in 1953, and was reprinted in succeeding years. The artwork features a young woman who is seated and holding a bottle of Coca-Cola, with a menu in front of her. The inner rim varies dramatically from that seen on trays previously issued by Coca-Cola. It shows a variety of sports scenes, and displays two slogans, including "Thirst Knows no Season" and "Have a Coke." Collectors have named this the "Menu Girl" tray for obvious reasons. The artwork also appeared on a version of the 1951 calendar. By far the most common of all Coca-Cola serving trays, the multiple issues of this tray undoubtedly numbered in the millions. Spanish and French versions of the tray were also produced. The Spanish variant has a red inner rim. Some additional minor variations of this tray have also been reported, and collectors may wish to search for them.

Beyond the "Menu Girl" tray, The Coca-Cola Company issued a serving tray in 1958 displaying a wicker basket pull cart stocked with food and Coca-Cola. The same art was used in 1956 on a "TV" tray. TV trays replaced the serving tray in the late fifties. With the booming growth of television in America's homes, a natural extension of the serving tray was the TV tray. Two TV tray issues in the late fifties demonstrated Coca-Cola's ability to adapt to changing times by making use of a functional advertising item that would appear prominently in the American home.

In addition to the 1950s trays issued for the American market, there were some trays issued for distribution throughout Canada in 1957. The most popular of these with collectors features a woman holding a bright umbrella and a bottle of Coca-Cola. Produced in English and French versions, this design is known as the "Umbrella Girl" tray. Three other Canadian tray designs were also issued in English and French language versions. One depicts a table displaying several servings of Coca-Cola and some sandwiches. Another shows a birdhouse next to a bottle of Coca-Cola; and yet another depicts flowers, a rooster, and a bottle of Coca-Cola.

This 11" by 14" cardboard sign featuring boxing great Sugar Ray Robinson is one of many signs used during the 1950s which showcased black entertainers and sports stars.

Although distributed only in Canada, many American collectors add these to their Coca-Cola tray collections.

While tray issues slowed dramatically in the forties and fifties, The Coca-Cola Company continued its incredible track record of growth. As was the case from the beginning, the firm demonstrated remarkable genius of innovation and resiliency in difficult times. The 1950s saw the introduction of still more creative packaging additions which would spark additional sales by giving customers more choices. The traditional 6 1/2-ounce bottle was supplemented by 10-, 12-, and 26-ounce bottles. By the end of the 1950s, the aluminum can was test marketed, and it would soon be introduced as a convenient container that would help Coca-Cola further broaden its ever-growing market.

THE SIXTIES

1961 marked the last official issue of a serving tray by The Coca-Cola Company. Known by collectors today as the "Pansy Garden" tray, it features artwork showing a bottle of Coca-Cola being poured into a glass, which is itself surrounded by colorful pansies. There are three American versions of the tray—each featuring different slogans. One version uses the slogan "Be Really Refreshed," while another uses two slogans which include "Coke Refreshes you Best" and "Here's a Coke for You." In addition, another "Be Really Refreshed" version exists which features an arciform-shaped Coca-Cola logo. This distinguishes it from other trays which used with the same slogan, but which display a rectangular logo. Thus, there are three variations of the "Pansy Garden" tray. In addition to copy changes, the tray was issued in Arabic, French-Canadian, and English-Canadian language variations.

Also in 1961, the company distributed a TV tray depicting a farm theme, with a table and flowers. All of the TV trays were produced in an 18 3/4-inch by 13 1/2-inch size. Additional TV tray designs were issued in Spanish versions only, in 1963 and 1969.

THE END OF A LONG CHAPTER IN COCA-COLA ADVERTISING HISTORY

The last serving trays offered by The Coca-Cola Company were distributed in the 1960s. After that time, trays would no longer be issued for the intended use of providing a vehicle for the soft drink to be served in soda fountains and restaurants. The serving tray had simply outlived its originally intended usefulness. While The Coca-Cola Company would later issue a series of reproduction trays in the 1970s for promotional purposes, these would not be distributed for soda fountain use.

As noted here, the first serving tray was issued in 1897, when Coca-Cola syrup was delivered by horse and buggy. In its closing chapter, the serving tray was witness to the early years of the space age, when America was planning a trip to the moon. In the period from 1896-1961, The Coca-Cola Company became—and remains—one of the world's most admired and resourceful companies. Serving tray artwork evolved with the times, and in doing so it chronicled the exciting and historical development of The Company. Whether you are a collector or simply someone interested in the history of The Coca-Cola Company, the remaining examples of these trays are true treasures that document the times of our parents and grandparents. In the eyes and minds of many, they reflect a time when life was more simple, and when a drink of Coca-Cola on a hot afternoon was a social event worth far more than the 5¢ that it cost for "the pause that refreshes."

1950 SERVING TRAY
PTR 052.000

After several years when no trays were produced, an issue which has become known to collectors as the "Girl with Wind in Hair" tray was distributed in 1950. The outer rim of the tray is silver and the inner rim is solid red. The tray was produced in a rectangular size measuring 10 3/8 inches by 13 1/4 inches. Unlike most of the trays issued by The Coca-Cola Company, there is no date or printer's name reflected on the tray. Two versions of the tray exist. The most common one (pictured here) has a graduated background surrounding the silhouette of the girl. The second version has a solid background. The solid, dark background version is the most difficult of the two to locate. A reproduction of this tray has also been produced. The original tray reveals much sharper and more distinct images and colors as compared to the reproduction.

1950 SERVING TRAY
VARIATION PTR 052.001

After several years when no trays were produced, an issue that has become known to collectors as the "Girl with Wind in Hair" tray was distributed in 1950. The outer rim of the tray is silver and the inner rim is solid red. The tray was produced in a rectangular size measuring 10 3/8 inches by 13 1/4 inches. Unlike most of the trays issued by The Coca-Cola Company, there is no date or printer's name shown on the tray. Two versions of the tray exist. The most common has a graduated background surrounding the silhouette of the girl. The second version has a solid, dark background. The solid, dark background version is the most difficult of the two to locate. This is the solid, dark background version of the 1950 tray.

1953 SERVING TRAY
PTR 053.000

Distributed beginning in 1953, and for several years following, this issue has become known as the "Menu Girl" tray because it depicts a young girl seated before a counter menu card, and holding a bottle of Coca-Cola. Instead of a red rim, the menu girl tray features a variety of sports themes on the inner rim. As with the 1950 tray, there is no mark designating the name of the printer. A very common tray, it is still desirable as an original tray issue. The tray was produced in a rectangular size measuring 10 5/8 inches by 13 1/4 inches. A Spanish version, with a red inner rim, was also produced.

1958 SERVING TRAY
PTR 054.000

The last 1950s tray produced for the U.S. market, known as the "Picnic Basket" tray, was issued in a 10 3/4-inch by 13 1/4-inch size. The tray was designed in a horizontal shape, and utilized the same artwork as a TV tray which was issued in the same year.

1957 CANADIAN SERVING TRAY
PTM 010.000

Coca-Cola also distributed four trays developed for distribution in the Canadian market. The most popular and scarce of the four is the "Girl with the Umbrella" or the "Umbrella" tray (above). The others include the "Sandwich Tray," (page 132) which shows sandwiches and Coca-Colas on a table in a horizontal tray design; the "Birdhouse Tray," (page 133) which shows a birdhouse scene; and the "Rooster Tray," (facing page) which shows a model of a rooster on a box, next to a bottle of Coca-Cola.

1957 CANADIAN SERVING TRAY
PTM 011.000

Although this tray depicts an interesting variety of objects, it is commonly known as the "Rooster Tray" in the collecting community. This particular tray was produced for, and distributed in, the Canadian market. Both English- and French-Canadian varieties of the tray were released.

1957 CANADIAN SERVING TRAY
PTM 012.000

This aptly-titled tray is known to the collecting community as the "Sandwich Tray." It depicts a tempting array of luncheon selections—accompanied, of course, by bottles of the delicious and refreshing Coca-Cola beverage. This tray was produced and distributed in the Canadian market, and it was made available in both English- and French-Canadian varieties.

1957 CANADIAN SERVING TRAY
PTM 013.000

The "Birdhouse Tray"—yet another example of a tray design where artwork inspired the title bestowed by the collecting community. Designed for distribution throughout the Canadian market, this tray, like most which were produced for that nation, was released in both English- and French-Candian versions.

1961 SERVING TRAY
PTR 055.001

The final issue of a tray produced as a promotional piece by The Coca-Cola Company was known as the "Pansy Garden" tray. Produced in a 10 1/4-inch by 13 3/4-inch size, the tray came in several versions which exhibit different slogans on the inner rim area. An Arabic version of this tray was also produced.

1956-1970 TV TRAYS
PTM 0013.000

With the diminishing use of the serving tray in the soda fountain, The Coca-Cola Company began to produce trays intended to be used in the new 1950s pastime of watching television in people's homes. Designed to fit on folding metal stands, these trays were produced to remind consumers that Coca-Cola was the perfect beverage to accompany food. The first TV tray was issued in 1956, with ten other issues known to have been distributed up through 1970.

1958 TV TRAY
PTM 0014.000

Beginning in 1958, as an indication of changing times, Coca-Cola produced TV trays advertising Coca-Cola. With an emphasis on consuming Coca-Cola in the home, this demonstrated the ability of the company to adapt innovative and highly effective ways to merchandise their product.

1961 TV TRAY
PTM 0016.000

During the early and mid 60s, the Coca-Cola Company produced several varieties of TV trays, including some in the Spanish language. This particular example uses a theme of Coca-Cola advertising of the 50s which tied Coca-Cola to All-American foods such as hamburgers, hot-dogs and picnic-type foods.

CHAPTER NINE

ESSENTIAL INFORMATION FOR COLLECTORS OF COCA-COLA TRAYS

Several reproduction trays were issued by The Coca-Cola Company in the 1970s. While minor identifiable alterations were added, such as placement of the trademark to differentiate reproductions from originals, new collectors are often fooled into thinking these are authentic originals. Another more insidious group of reproductions have been made without the permission of The Coca-Cola Company. Perhaps the most common of these is the 1934 Weissmuller tray reproduction, which is often represented as an original and sold to uninitiated collectors who think they are getting "a deal." To the untrained eye, this can lead to a very costly mistake. The novice collector should become informed on the subject by reading all available materials and seeking direction from knowledgeable collectors— BEFORE BUYING. Reproduction trays, along with other contemporary "created collectibles," are not recommended as investment items. Reproductions simply cannot be compared with original Coca-Coca advertising. Original production Coca-Cola trays are true antiques, and will always be valued additions to a collection. Reproductions, on the other hand, are just that—reproductions.

Following are some guidelines to observe in evaluating serving trays, and to help you determine which have been reproduced and which have not.

Printer Marks: Most of the original serving and change trays bear the name of the firm that printed them. Those which do not display the printer's name include trays designated for the years 1897, 1899, 1920, 1921, and trays issued after 1950. Another tray which has not been specifically dated, and which also does not include a printer's mark, is the "Topless" tray, thought to have been distributed after 1905. Reproduction trays do not display the printer's name.

Printing Quality: None of the reproduction trays have the clarity, color, or brightness of the originals. It is advisable for new collectors to seek the assistance of a knowledgeable and experienced collector in studying, firsthand, a quality collection of original trays. This type of exposure is necessary to fully understand and appreciate the subtle variations between reproductions and originals.

Buying Sources: Nothing beats doing business with knowledgeable dealers and collectors whose primary motto is integrity. As with any collectible, enlightenment is supreme. Check price guides, talk to collectors, and most of all, be discerning in your search for quality trays.

COLLECTING COCA-COLA TRAYS

Few collectibles can match the fascination and breadth of history that results from assembling a collection of original Coca-Cola trays. For the many who cannot afford a complete collection of trays, accumulating the red-rim tray series (1926-1950) offers an exciting challenge. Certainly, one could also select a favorite decade of trays to collect, or perhaps one each of the "swimsuit" girls. Another enjoyable way to collect trays would be to select the ones that had matching calendars and obtain both the calendar and the corresponding tray for the same year. The possibilities are endless. Many of the trays in high-grade condition are underpriced, relative to how difficult they are to locate. Several of the trays from the 1920s and 1930s list for under $700 in price guides, but are difficult to locate in investment-quality condition. As with all antique advertising, CONDITION is paramount to value. For this reason, a mint or very nearly mint condition tray may sell for three or more times what a well-worn example of the same issue will bring. Following are some important points to keep in mind relating to collecting and preserving Coca-Cola serving trays, or, for that matter, other metal signs and antique advertising memorabilia items.

Where to buy Coca-Cola Memorabilia: Historical Coca-Cola advertising is available from many different sources, including antique shows, shops, auctions, and through ads in various antiques publications such as the *Antique Trader*. Some of the greatest finds have come from yard and garage sales. Another source is through the Coca-Cola Collectors Club, which is an international organization of people dedicated to the study and collection of Coca-Cola memorabilia. The club publishes a monthly newsletter known as *The Coca-Cola Collectors News*, which features a large classified section wherein serving trays are often offered for sale.

Grading: Properly ascertaining the condition or grade of an antique advertising piece is critical to making a reasoned purchase decision. Undoubtedly, many readers have heard the expression, "It's like new if you consider how old it is." Always remember that the first trays looked fabulous when printed, and were totally new in appearance. Age doesn't change the parameters of grading. It's possible to find rare examples of trays produced from 1900-1910 that are just as pristine in appearance as the nicest available example of the 1941 "skater girl." Mint is mint! Age doesn't allow for any slackening of grading standards. Before purchasing a serving tray that is promoted at a certain grade, always assure yourself that the tray has been properly described and categorized. If and when you may eventually wish to sell the item, you can be sure that the next potential buyer won't understand, or care, that you bought an improperly graded piece. He or she will only care about the actual condition (grading) at the time when the tray is offered for sale. A tray grading and scarcity guide is included in this book. Please take the time to read it carefully. Knowledge rules supreme when buying antique advertising. This book provides the tools to help avoid costly mistakes.

Trading and Upgrading: Many collectors start collecting with a level of quality expectation that may evolve over the years. Generally, as one learns more about a field of collecting, tastes become more discriminating. Serving trays offer a wonderful opportunity to improve and upgrade quality over a period of time. As significantly better examples of trays are spotted in the course of collecting, the collector has the option of upgrading and selling the lesser tray to help defray the expense of the better, more expensive tray. In this way, one can gradually build a very high-quality collection of trays.

Displaying Trays: The most common way to hang and display trays is to use tray magnets which are readily available from advertising dealers. Tray magnets are nailed to the wall with the magnet side out, and the trays are simply affixed to them. While one magnet would probably suffice, using two per tray will insure that the trays cannot be easily jarred off the wall. Do not use plate hangers with metal hooks that attach to the rims of the trays. Perfect mint trays have been subsequently scratched by the use of metal plate holders. Another desirable method of displaying trays is to build a special wall shelf with notched grooves that will hold the trays in place. Both methods work equally well. In any case, you should store the trays in a

The Coca-Cola Company actively encouraged its customers to promote its product with a dazzling array of fabulous advertising art. This 1920s soda fountain was a good example of how effectively the company's merchandising collateral was used to promote Coca-Cola.

place where they won't fall off the wall, and where they aren't exposed to extended periods of sunlight or florescent light—both of which will cause irreparable fading over a period of time.

Cleaning and Maintenance: The best way to preserve trays is to keep them original. Cleaning won't restore color that has been lost to exposure to light, or repair scratches due to wear and tear. If a tray is dirty or filmy, basic warm water and a soft, non-abrasive cloth are the best cleaning tools to use. Waxing trays can either improve them or damage them. If one must wax a tray, a non-abrasive carnuba wax and very soft cloths should be used. Ordinary cleaning waxes have microscopic grit and sand that can dull and damage the surface of a tray. Lacquering a tray is never recommended. In time, many of today's lacquers will yellow on the surface of a tray. Do keep in mind, however, that original trays did have a protective lacquer coat applied as a final stage of the printing process.

Restoration: For some of the truly rare trays, restoration may be a viable alternative when the expense of finding a high-grade example is prohibitive, or when finding such an example is nearly impossible due to lack of availability. There are several important factors to be weighed when considering restoration. First, it isn't worth the expense to professionally restore the more common trays. Second, improper restoration of a tray will do more damage than good. Quality restorers are few and far between. Talk to a knowledgeable dealer to find out who handles museum-quality restorations. Also, plan on waiting a very long time for your tray to be restored—top restorers have more work than they can handle. Also, remember that a restored tray must always be represented as such in any future dealings. Failure to disclose restoration at the time of sale is unethical!

Tray Variations: Minor variations often occur among tray issues. For example, the 1940 tray was issued with both a silver and a gold outer-edged rim. Other trays were issued in foreign language versions. To date, the variations have not proven as collectible as the more prevalent designs, but they are worth noting and collecting by the advanced collector. This book has detailed many of the existing and known variations, but there are undoubtedly others that will surface in the future.

Serving Trays as Investments: Over time, high-quality original Coca-Cola serving trays have proven to be outstanding investments. In the past three or four years, many tray issues in high-grade condition have doubled and even tripled in price. How many other collectibles offer the opportunity to display a beautiful array of artwork in one's home, while achieving investment objectives as well? Even if the major purpose of collecting serving trays isn't for investment purposes, it is reassuring to know that this is a hobby that can prove to be profitable. Of course, there is no guarantee regarding what will happen in the future, but if current trends continue, the investment aspect of accumulating serving trays is worth considering.

SOME FINAL THOUGHTS

This book has provided an account of the development of The Coca-Cola Company and the role advertising trays played in promoting the most well-known soft drink in the world. While the primary purpose of the book is to provide collectors of Coca-Cola advertising memorabilia with valuable information, one cannot help but be fascinated by the exciting history of The Coca-Cola Company itself. We are fortunate today to find examples of these serving trays in collections and museums, but the search is by no means over. Somewhere, in the attic of an old house or in the basement of an old country store, there are undoubtedly yet more treasures to be found. Was there an as-yet-undiscovered tray issued in 1896 or 1898? Where is that complete box of fifty brand new, mint condition, 1932 serving trays in fresh-from-the-printer condition? Each year, new discoveries of old, original Coca-Cola memorabilia are made. As with any pursuit in life, the journey is often more rewarding than the destination.

PVA 006.000

CHAPTER TEN

VIENNA ART PLATES

Although never intended to serve the same purpose as Coca-Cola serving trays, Vienna art plates have become collectible as a related category. Designed and patented just after the turn of the century, these advertising pieces were metal plates with printed illustrations of a variety of subjects—predominantly attractive women.

On February 21, 1905, a patent was granted to the H. D. Beach Company of Coshocton, Ohio, for the "Beach Metal Plaque." Beach called his new invention "Vienna Art Plates." Subsequent to Beach offering this new product to merchandisers, several other advertising tin lithographers introduced similar products. Chas. W. Shonk Co. offered the Royal Saxony Art Plate; Meek Co., the Dresden Art Plate; Kaufmann & Strauss, the K & S Plate; and Bachrach & Co., the Bachrach Plate. These products were produced through the mid-teens.

Shaped exactly like a dining plate, with diameters of 10 inches to 10 1/4 inches, Vienna Art Plates were designed to be decorative display pieces. H. D. Beach's first art plates depicted the European art of Wagner and A. Asti, who were well-known artists with a talent for painting pictures of beautiful women. Ironically, few of the art plates produced by the various tin lithographers had advertising on the front of the plate. Instead, the reference to the advertiser was imprinted on the back of the plate.

Some of these plates were surrounded with ornate gold frames. A still smaller number were sold by the manufacturer in glass-covered shadow boxes. Art plates found in the original frames and shadow boxes are especially desirable, and are worth more than plates without them.

The tie-in of these interesting and odd advertising art plates to The Coca-Cola Company is an unusual story. Never purchased or authorized by The Company headquarters in Atlanta, these items were procured for distribution by the Western Coca-Cola Bottling Company in Chicago. This particular regional bottler's territory included Chicago and the Western States and, over the years, most examples of the Vienna Art Plates have turned up in these areas. What is so unique about these plates is that they had virtually no real advertising value. The viewer of the art plate

Back of Art Plate showing "Vienna Art Plate" mark. It is important to note that these are "stock" plates and can be found with other advertising on the back. Plates found without Coca-Cola on the back are not considered as a Coca-Cola collectible.

would have needed to study the back of the piece to determine just who made the item. Undoubtedly, they were given away more on a complimentary basis to customers than with the specific intent of actually advertising Coca-Cola. In the case of the Coca-Cola issues, the back of the plate reads as follows:

VIENNA ART PLATES Patent. Feb. 21st 1905 Western Coca-Cola Bottling Co. Chicago, Ill.

A total of eight issues of the Vienna Art Plates are known to exist with the Western Coca-Cola Bottling Co. designation on their back. All picture beautiful women, and several of them are somewhat risqué in that they reflect partially nude ladies. It is likely that these were meant to be hung in saloons where Coca-Cola was used as a mixer for cocktails. One example bears exactly the same artwork, without any advertising, as the "Topless" tray which was also distributed by The Western Coca-Cola Bottling Company. It is also possible that other, as yet undiscovered, issues of the Vienna Art Plates were distributed.

As is the case with the serving trays, condition and rarity determine value. As noted previously, art plates in original frames and with shadow boxes in pristine condition are worth more than those without these features. Individually, the art plate with the same picture as the "Topless" tray is the most sought after.

Collectors wanting to learn more about Vienna Art Plates and other similar products from tin lithographers from the period 1905-1915 can gain more detailed information from *Hazelcorns Price Guide to Tin Vienna Art Plates*, by Jane and Howard Hazelcorn, which was published in 1987.

PVA 001.000

PVA 002.00

PVA 003.000

PVA 004.000

PVA 005.000

PVA 007.000

PVA 008.000

With a massive promotional budget in the teens years, Coca-Cola used ads like this in national publications. This ad shows the same image as the oblong 1916 tray, but in a round design not known to have been issued.

CHAPTER ELEVEN

COCA-COLA SERVING AND CHANGE TRAY RARITY OVERVIEW

U nlike coinage produced by the United States Mint, we do not know the exact number of serving trays issued from year to year by The Coca-Cola Company. We do have some reliable estimates of the numbers of trays distributed during the years 1906 to 1910, and also in 1913, based on records of purchases from the various tin lithographers who printed the items. Beyond that, there is no precise accounting for the actual numbers of trays issued. Consequently, estimating the scarcity and availability of the various tray issues is not an exact science. Lacking evidence either supporting or disproving the existence of various serving and change trays, or documentation which verifies their scarcity, we must rely on the knowledge of experts in the field who have bought and sold Coca-Cola advertising memorabilia for many years.

The attrition rate of serving and change trays has proven to be tremendous. It is unlikely that even one percent of the trays originally produced exist today in any condition. And, in the case of trays issued in the earliest years of the Coca-Cola Company, the number is far less than that.

It was in the 1960s that significant numbers of collectors began to actively seek Coca-Cola advertising memorabilia. Individuals interested in antique advertising and Coca-Cola items became increasingly aware of serving trays and their availability (or scarcity), and in the period from 1960-1995, these items traded hands at numerous sales, auctions, and antique shows. Of those available, many ended up in a few major private collections, where they may still reside.

Trays are often collected in a series. For instance, some collectors specialize in the red-rim tray series issued from 1926-1950. Others collect only change trays, while those with dynamic financial resources may attempt to collect the entire series. Consequently, the scarcity guide presented here will be broken down into the following categories:

- All Change Tray issues from 1900 to 1920
- All Serving Tray issues from 1897 to 1953
- The red-rim Serving Tray issues from 1926 to 1950

COCA-COLA TRAY SCARCITY GUIDE

The following rarity index lists trays in descending order, from most rare (at the top of the list) to more commonly seen or available (at the bottom). There are varieties of a few of these trays in which minor and insignificant differences exist, but these distinctions are incidental to the design. The rarity index presented here covers the major designs and issues, with only important variations noted.

Change Trays Issued from 1900 to 1920

1903	Bottle (very rare!)
1900	Hilda Clark
1901	Hilda Clark
1903	Hilda Clark, 4 1/8" diameter
1903	Hilda Clark, 6" diameter
1906	Juanita
1907	Relieves Fatigue
1910	The Coca-Cola Girl
1909	Exibition Girl
1920	Golfer Girl
1913	Hamilton King Girl
1914	Betty*
1916	Girl with a Basket of Flowers*

Serving Trays Issued from 1897 to 1953

1897	Victorian Girl Tray*
1899	Hilda
1903	Bottle
1907	Relieves Fatigue, Large Oval
1900	Hilda*
1901	Hilda
1903	Hilda, Large Oval
1909	Exhibition Girl, Large Oval
1903	Round
1906	Juanita
1907	Relieves Fatigue, Small Oval
1905	Lillian Nordica, with Bottle
1905	Lillian Nordica, with Glass
1905-1908	Topless
1909	Exhibition Girl, Small Oval
1910	The Coca-Cola Girl*
1913	Hamilton King, Oval
1912	Hamilton King, Rectangular*
1929	Girl in the Yellow Bathing Suit, with Bottle (Tindeco)

1924	Smiling Girl (brown and red-rim versions)
1927	Curb Service
1921	Autumn Girl
1920	Golfer Girl, Large Oval
1920	Golfer Girl
1932	Girl in Bathing Suit
1928	Bobbed Hair Girl
1926	Golfing Couple*
1922	Summer Girl
1933	Frances Dee
1929	Girl in Yellow Bathing Suit, with Glass
1927	Soda Jerk
1950	Girl With Wind in Hair, dark-green background
1934	Weissmuller*
1930	Bather Girl
1931	Barefoot Boy, or Rockwell
1914	Betty, Oval*
1916	Girl With a Basket of Flowers*
1914	Betty Rectangular
1923	Flapper Girl*
1925	Party Girl*
1935	Madge Evans
1930	Telephone Girl
1936	Hostess
1937	Running Girl
1939	Springboard Girl
1940	Sailor Girl
1938	Girl at Shade
1942	Two Girls at Car
1941	Skater Girl
1950	Girl with Wind in Hair, light-green background*
1953	Menu Girl

Red Rim Tray Series (1926-1950)

1929	Swimsuit Girl, with Bottle (Tindeco)
1927	Curb Service
1932	Girl In Bathing Suit
1928	Bobbed Hair Girl
1926	Golfing Couple*
1933	Frances Dee
1929	Girl In Yellow Bathing Suit (glass version)
1950	Girl With Wind in Hair, dark-green background
1927	Soda Jerk
1934	Weissmuller*

*INDICATES TRAYS WHICH HAVE BEEN REPRODUCED

1930	Bather Girl
1931	Barefoot Boy or Rockwell
1935	Madge Evans
1930	Telephone Girl
1936	Hostess
1937	Running Girl*
1939	Springboard Girl
1940	Sailor Girl
1938	Girl at Shade
1942	Two Girls at Car
1941	Skater Girl
1950	Girl with Wind in Hair*

*INDICATES TRAYS WHICH HAVE BEEN REPRODUCED

(please note disclaimer below)

Disclaimer: The authors have included information in this book related to tray reproductions they are aware of. The above list may not be all inclusive, and other reproductions may exist. Also, it's possible that other new reproductions may be produced at some time after this book has been published.

Although every effort has been made to provide accurate and precise information in these listings, the authors are not responsible for any errors or omissions which may be contained herein.

COCA-COLA TRAY PRICE GUIDE

The following price guide lists all of the Coca-Cola trays and Vienna Art Plates currently known to exist. In order to assist the collector and dealer, prices have been categorized into three distinct grades. Over the years, the grading of antique advertising signs and trays has evolved toward the use of numerical descriptions. In the case of advertising trays, prices vary widely, based on condition. For example, in today's market, a 1942 Coca-Cola tray might well bring as much as $475 if it is in "new old stock" or mint condition. Conversely, one with considerable wear, detracting marks, or fading, but nevertheless presenting a displayable picture, would probably sell for $100. To quantify that difference, we have provided a definition of common numerical grades.

Years ago, when the value range between a mint condition tray and a well-worn tray was relatively small, grading was not particularly critical. The previously noted example of the 1942 tray explains why it is so important to properly grade trays in today's market. The mint example of a 1942 tray generally sells for four or more times what one in well-worn condition would bring. For this reason, the use of numbers in grading is helpful. Using a scale of 1-10, a tray can be described in all states of condition, from virtually destroyed and not displayable to new or mint condition.

For purposes of this grading guide, we have provided descriptions which will allow the collector to understand grading terms used by most dealers and serious collectors. The price guide lists grading descriptions in the grades 7.5, 8.5, and 9.5 on a scale of ten. These grades cover a range from what is minimally collectible (7.5), collectible and nicely displayable (8.5), to near-mint-plus condition (9.5). The price guide does not include specific grading descriptions of trays in less than 75% of new (or 7.5 on a scale of 10) condition. Trays in lesser condition are not considered desirable or collectible unless they are very early and extremely rare issues where only a few known examples exist (for example, the 1899 tray would be valuable in any condition).

Various types of grading systems have been used over the years to describe the condition of antique advertising and serving trays. Most guides list conditions ranging from "good" to "very good" to "fine" to "excellent" to "near mint" and ultimately to "mint" condition. The problem with this type of terminology is that what is described as a tray in "good" condition is, in reality, a tray or advertising piece that is faded, worn, and damaged. It is, therefore, more practical and useful to describe antiques via a numerical grading scale, with the number "10" depicting perfection, or an item that is in new and unused condition. Some refer to mint condition as "new old stock," meaning that the item is old, but is in mint condition.

Numbers less than 10 refer to trays that show various states of wear or handling. Many antique dealers, and some collectors, use optimistic grading, or what could be more appropriately termed "overgrading." We often hear the expression that a given item is in wonderful condition "if you consider how old it is." Such expressions should cause immediate concern to the buyer. Near-mint examples of some of the very earliest trays produced are known to exist, discounting the notion that age always equates with a somewhat deteriorated condition. As we noted earlier, condition is not qualified by age! The following are the numerical equivalents that match grading terminology used to describe antique advertising over the years:

Grade Description	Numerical Equivalent
Mint Condition	10
Near Mint Plus	9.5-9.9
Near Mint	9.0-9.4
Excellent to Excellent Plus	8.5-8.9
Excellent Minus	8.0-8.5
Collectible/Displayable, but showing moderate to considerable visible wear	7.0-7.5

10—MINT CONDITION: Although this grade is not used for pricing in this price guide, it is important as a reference point. A mint tray is New Old Stock or PERFECT. That means as-printed at time of manufacture—no flaws, no rim rubs—a tray possessing unblemished surfaces with mint-fresh shine and color. In a word: perfect! In actuality, few if any trays are found in this condition. The authors have seen many trays which are New Old Stock trays, but even these have minor blemishes or tiny marks on the rim. Most trays customarily graded in new condition should probably be more accurately graded at 9.8 or 9.9 on a scale of 10. Mint condition, and trays which are just a hair's breath from being perfect, are the ultimate collectibles. They bring whatever the market will bear when they are offered for sale.

9.5—NEAR MINT++ CONDITION: Trays in this state of preservation must exhibit very few handling marks or wear. At a distance of one to two feet, such trays will display a nearly perfect appearance. Trays deserving this lofty grade must have mint-fresh colors, a high shine (although minor crazing* is acceptable), and no more than a couple of rim rubs, or perhaps a few very minor flaws (not readily visible) in the picture. Trays found in this condition were probably never used for their intended purpose, and any minor imperfections they have probably resulted from some minimal handling over the years, or as a result of the manufacturing process. In early and scarce issues of trays, this grade is not easily attainable. Conversely, trays issued after 1937 were produced in large quantities, and they do become available in this grade from time to time.

8.5—EXCELLENT CONDITION: This grade is commonly accepted by tray collectors who desire a nice tray, but do not wish to spend the significant sum necessary to purchase one in near mint condition. Trays in excellent or 8.5 condition must exhibit bright original colors with a moderate shine. They may display some rim rubs, but most areas of the raised rim must be intact and undamaged. Trays in this grade may also have minor scratches or marks on the picture and inside the rim, but none may be large or easily noticeable. Overall, a tray in this grade must exhibit an appearance which is very pleasing and attractive to display. Trays with fading, or sizeable flaws such as a cigarette burn or scratches that noticeably deter from the tray's general appearance, do not qualify at this grade. All in all, an 8.5 is a very nice tray, but one which just does not qualify for the near mint rating.

7.5—COLLECTIBLE CONDITION: A tray grading 7.5 on a scale of 10 would exhibit some of the following detractions: significant rim rubs, fading and color loss, a dent or two, wear on the surface of the picture, and/or marks or small spots here and there. Still, to attain this collectible grade, the tray must have virtually all of the original image intact, and exhibit a displayable appearance. This grade is collectible in early and rare trays, but is less desirable in more commonly available issues.

*Crazing is a condition caused by heat and cold variations. Trays were sometimes stored in warehouses and buildings which were subject to significant temperature changes from day to night. Such temperature changes caused expansion and contraction of the clear surface coat, resulting in a spider web appearance on the top surface of the tray. This phenomenon does not usually affect the overall condition or appearance of the tray. Some trays that exhibit this checking appearance are otherwise in nearly perfect condition. Crazing often appears on early trays produced in the first part of the century. Wear and handling do not contribute to crazing.

CHANGE TRAYS

ISSUE	GRADE 7.5	GRADE 8.5	GRADE 9.5
1900 Hilda Clark, 6"	$1,700	$4,500	$5,500
1901 Hilda Clark, 6"	$1,500	$2,800	$4,000
1903 Hilda Clark, 6"	$900	$1,800	$3,000
1903 Hilda Clark, 4"	$1,000	$2,600	$3,400
1903 Bottle, 5 1/2"	$2,800	$8,000	$9,500
1906 Juanita, 4"	$350	$900	$1,300
1907 Relieves Fatigue	$400	$850	$1,500
1909 Exhibition Girl	$225	$650	$850
1910 Coca-Cola Girl	$225	$750	$950
1913 Hamilton King Girl	$225	$600	$850
1914 Betty	$75	$325	$425
1916 Girl With Flowers	$75	$275	$350
1920 Golfer Girl	$200	$475	$650

SERVING TRAYS

ISSUE	GRADE 7.5	GRADE 8.5	GRADE 9.5
1897 Victorian Girl	$15,000	$25,000	$45,000
1899 Hilda Clark	$10,000	$15,000	$25,000
1900 Hilda Clark	$7,500	$9,000	$12,000
1901 Hilda Clark	$3,500	$7,500	$9,500
1903 Hilda Clark (round)	$2,200	$7,000	$9,500
1903 Hilda Clark (large oval)	$3,500	$6,500	$9,000
1903 Bottle Tray	$5.000	$8,000	$13,000
1905 Nordica Bottle and Glass Versions	$2,000	$4,800	$6,500
1906 Juanita	$2,000	$3,500	$5,000
1907 Relieves Fatigue (small oval)	$2,200	$3,800	$4,800
1907 Relieves Fatigue (large oval)	$2,600	$6,000	$7,500
1905-07 Topless	$3,500	$6,500	$11,000
1909 Exibition Girl (small oval)	$1,200	$2,800	$3,500
1909 Exhibition Girl (large oval)	$1,500	$4,000	$5,500
1910 Coca-Cola Girl	$450	$1,600	$2,100
1913 Hamilton King (large oval)	$450.00	$800.00	$1,300
1913 Hamilton King (rectangle)	$350	$950	$1,200
1914 Betty (oval)	$275	$650	$850
1914 Betty (rectangle)	$225	$900	$1,200
1916 Girl with Basket of Flowers	$225	$500	$675
1920 Golfer Girl (oval)	$300	$950	$1,700
1920 Golfer Girl (rectangle)	$300	$1,100	$1,500
1921 Autumn Girl	$300	$1,100	$1,400

ISSUE	GRADE 7.5	GRADE 8.5	GRADE 9.5
1922 Summer Girl	$300	$950	$1,500
1923 Flapper Girl	$250	$550	$700
1924 Smiling Girl (maroon rim)	$325	$1,200	$1,500
1924 Smiling Girl (brown rim)	$325	$800	$1,500
1925 Party Girl	$200	$575	$725
1926 Golfing Couple	$300	$1,000	$1,500
1927 Curb Service	$300	$950	$1,800
1927 Soda Jerk	$275	$900	$1,150
1928 Bobbed-Hair Girl	$275	$900	$1,250
1929 Girl in Bathing Suit (bottle)	$325	$750	$1,500
1929 Girl in Bathing Suit (glass)	$250	$600	$1,150
1930 Swimsuit Girl	$200	$600	$950
1930 Telephone Girl	$175	$550	$650
1931 Rockwell	$350	$1,000	$1,450
1932 Swimsuit Girl	$300	$900	$1,450
1933 Frances Dee	$275	$750	$1,350
1934 Weissmuller	$350	$1,000	$1,450
1935 Madge Evans	$175	$475	$650
1936 Hostess	$125	$450	$750
1937 Running Girl	$110	$350	$450
1938 Girl at Shade	$100	$275	$350
1939 Springboard Girl	$100	$350	$385
1940 Sailor Girl	$100	$350	$385

ISSUE	GRADE 7.5	GRADE 8.5	GRADE 9.5
1941 Skater Girl	$100	$385	$425
1942 Two Girls at Car	$100	$385	$425
1950 Girl with Wind in Hair (regular version)	$35	$75	$125
1950 Girl with Wind in Hair (green background)	$250	$400	$575
1953 Menu Girl	$25	$60	$75
1957 Rooster	$35	$175	$195
1957 Umbrella Girl	$150	$300	$425
1957 Sandwich Tray	$25	$150	$165
1958 Wagon	$1	$40	$45
1961 Pansy Tray	$10	$30	$35

VIENNA ART PLATES

(without frame, and refer to The Coca-Cola Company on the back)

PLATE ISSUE	GRADE 7.5	GRADE 8.5	GRADE 9.5
(Petretti reference: pva001.000)	$275	$700	$1,000
(Petretti reference: pva002.000)	$125	$275	$375
(Petretti reference: pva003.000)	$125	$325	$425
(Petretti reference: pva004.000)	$125	$325	$425
(Petretti reference: pva005.000)	$125	$325	$425
(Petretti reference: pva006.000)	$200	$600	$850
(Petretti reference: pva007.000)	$200	$325	$425
(Petretti reference: pva008.000)	$275	$600	$1,000

Vienna Art Plates with original ornate gold frames bring double or more the value of unframed examples. Add as much as fifty percent to framed value if they are also in their original glass shadow boxes.

Editor's note: Grade 8.5 values for trays and Vienna art plates correspond to Petretti values for items in excellent condition as noted in *Petretti's Coca-Cola Collectibles Price Guide*, 10th edition.

BIBLIOGRAPHY

BOOKS

Hazelcorn, Jane and Howard. *Hazelcorn's Price Guide to Tin Vienna Art Plates.*
New Jersey: H. J. H. Publications, 1987.

Hoy, Anne. *Coca-Cola: The First Hundred Years.* Georgia: The Coca-Cola
Company, 1986.

Muzio, Jack. *Collectable Tin Advertising Trays.* California: Jack Muzio, 1971.

Palazzini, Fioria Steinbach. *Coca-Cola Superstar.* New Zealand: Barrons
Educational Series, Inc., in assoc. with David Bateman Ltd. "Golden Heights," 1988.

Petretti, Allan. *Petretti's Coca-Cola Collectibles Price Guide*-10th Edition.
Dubuque, Iowa: Antique Trader Books, 1997.

Schmidt, Bill and Jan. *The Schmidt Museum Collection of Coca-Cola
Memorabilia.* Kentucky: Schmidt Books, 1983.

Strang, Lewis C. *Famous Prima Donnas.* Massachusetts: L. C. Page & Co., 1900.

PERIODICALS, BROCHURES, AND IMPORTANT DOCUMENTS

Coca-Cola Bottlers Current Advertising Price List. Several of these annual issues
for Coca-Cola bottlers were used in developing this publication. These catalogs contained pictures and prices of advertising materials available to bottlers from The
Coca-Cola Company.

Garrett, Franklin. *The Black Book/History of Coca-Cola 1886-1940.* Coca-Cola
Archives. Franklin Garrett was Company Historian in the Public Relations
Department when this history was compiled in 1940. Unpublished.

Minutes of The Coca-Cola Company. Coca-Cola Company Archives. 1905-1919.
Unpublished.

The Coca-Cola Bottler. First published in April 1909, this monthly publication
was developed by The Coca-Cola Company for the bottler. Much information about
early merchandising is contained in issues of The Coca-Cola Bottler, and this material was used in preparation of this book.

The Red Barrel. First published in January of 1926, this monthly publication was issued by The Coca-Cola Company for fountain service customers. Numerous articles and pictures from a variety of these monthly publications were used for this book.

"The Rise of the American Prima Donna." *Munsey's Magazine*. 1901.

The Chronicle of Coca-Cola since 1886. Published by The Coca-Cola Company.

RESEARCH NOTES

Information for this reference book came from a variety of published and unpublished sources. Significant historical data about The Coca-Cola Company was obtained from The Coca-Cola Archives in Atlanta. Estimates of scarcity of certain issues of Serving and Change trays are derived from the authors' combined 30+ years of collecting, buying, and selling Coca-Cola advertising memorabilia. Both authors have purchased, bought, auctioned, and sold hundreds of serving trays over the years. Additionally, the authors have viewed, and derived invaluable information and insights from, several major collections of Coca-Cola serving and change trays.

ABOUT THE AUTHORS

ALLAN PETRETTI

Being in the printing and advertising business with an interest in history provided a natural opportunity for Allan Petretti to become interested in collecting the advertising of The Coca-Cola Company. By the early 1970s, he was a devoted collector and was among the early groups of organized collectors. A member of The Coca-Cola Collectors' Club, he created, organized, and conducted the first club auction at the San Diego convention in 1978. Beginning in 1976, he published his first mail-bid auction. Twenty-one years and forty-two auctions later, these semi-annual auctions have become one of the main sources of quality Coca-Cola and other soda-pop memorabilia, selling over 52,000 pieces.

Petretti's Coca-Cola Collectible Price Guide, now in its 10th edition, is not only considered the "bible" to most collectors, but has also become the standard which many other price guides follow. Petretti's Soda-Pop Collectible Price Guide, published in 1996, is the only book dealing with the entire soda-pop collectibles field.

Allan Petretti's many appearances on nationally syndicated television and radio shows include "Personal FX," "Smart Money with the Dolans," "Watchagot" with Harry Rinker, and "Rinker on Collectibles." In addition, he is a regular talk show guest on radio stations nationwide. Mr. Petretti also writes a regular column for the Antique Trader Weekly, Gameroom Magazine, *as well as writing feature articles for a number of antique publications. He also does seminars around the country for Coca-Cola Collectors' groups. Mr.*

Petretti also has been interviewed by The Wall Street Journal, USA Today, The Robb Report, (Investibles), *and collectible columnists from all over the country. He is also called upon to conduct appraisals for insurance companies and private collections.*

Writing on Coca-Cola collectibles, as well as buying and selling on a full-time basis, Mr. Petretti has become one of the nation's foremost authorities on values and market trends of Coca-Cola memorabilia.

CHRIS H. BEYER

Chris H. Beyer resides in the Atlanta, Georgia, area with his wife Gina and five children. Mr. Beyer and his wife began collecting Coca-Cola serving trays in 1984. Since that time they have become avid collectors of advertising memorabilia in general. Combining a love of antiques with an interest in the historical development of printed promotional advertising materials, Mr. Beyer has written articles for Collector's Showcase *and* The Inside Collector *magazines. In the past few years, he has spent an enormous amount of time researching the historical development of advertising and promotion by The Coca-Cola Company.*

Interest in advertising and merchandising comes naturally to Mr. Beyer, who is employed as the national marketing manager for a major building products corporation. In that capacity he does extensive professional writing and has authored various newsletters and articles for several national business trade publications. He wishes to dedicate this book to his wife and children who lovingly support his endeavors as an author and collector.

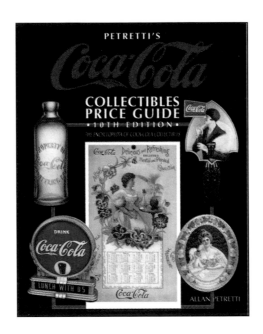